John
of flight.
resen$ 20.75

THE WORLD'S GREATEST AIRCRAFT

THE CHRONOLOGY OF FLIGHT

1940 to the Present

THE WORLD'S GREATEST AIRCRAFT
THE CHRONOLOGY OF FLIGHT

1940 to the Present

Michael J.H.Taylor

Chelsea House Publishers • Philadelphia

Published in 2000 by
Chelsea House Publishers
1974 Sproul Road, Suite 400
P.O. Box 914
Broomall. PA, 19008-0914

ISBN 0-7910-5424-1

Printed in China

Library of Congress Cataloging-in-Publication Data

Taylor, Michael John Haddrick.
     The chronology of flight. 1940 to the present / Michael
J.H. Taylor
          p.   cm. -- (The world's greatest aircraft)
     Published simultaneously: The chronology 1940--
present. London:
     Includes index.
     Summary: An illustrated chronology of the important
dates in the history of flight and aircraft. from 1940 to the
present.
     ISBN 0-7910-5424-1 (hc.)
     1. Aeronautics Chronology Juvenile literature. [1.
Aeronautics Chronology.] I. Title. II. Series.
TL547.T38   1999
629.13'02'02--do21
                                                        99-25902
                                                        CIP

Airbus A3XX is expected to enter service in 2004 as the world's first full double-deck very-high-capacity commercial long-range airliner

1940

January 1 The first flight is recorded of the Yakovlev I-26 (Yak-1) prototype, a design which leads to a valuable and closely related family of Yakovlev fighters to be used by the Soviet air force throughout the Second World War.

February 14 A Lockheed Hudson of R.A.F. Coastal Command locates the German prison ship *Altmark* in Norwegian territorial waters.

February 22 Sqdn. Ldr. Douglas Farquhar of No. 602 (City of Glasgow) Squadron, Auxiliary Air Force, takes the first British gun-camera film of the war while attacking and destroying a Heinkel He 111 over Coldingham, Berwickshire.

February 22/23 Luftwaffe He 111s accidentally bomb German naval vessels during Operation *Wikinger*. The destroyers *Lebrecht Maas* and *Max Schultz* run into a British minefield and are lost.

February 24 First flight of the Hawker Typhoon prototype (P5212) powered by a Napier-Sabre II engine.

February 25 The first unit of the Royal Canadian Air Force arrives in the U.K.

February 26 The United States War Department forms the U.S. Air Defense Command to integrate defences against possible attack from the air.

March 12 Overwhelmed by the sheer weight of the Soviet attack, Finland capitulates to its invaders.

March 25 U.S.A.A.C. contractors are authorized to sell to anti-Axis governments modern types of Army combat aircraft. This is seen as a means of expanding production facilities to the future benefit of the U.S.A.A.C. should the U.S.A. become involved in war.

March 30 First flight of the Lavochkin I-22 or LaGG-1 fighter, from which is developed an improved LaGG-3, to be used extensively by the Soviet Air Force during the early stages of the German invasion.

April 5 The first flight is made of the Mikoyan and Gurevich MiG-1 prototype, built in comparatively small production numbers before development of the improved MiG-3. (q.v. August, 1940)

April 13 The first anti-shipping mines of the war to be air-dropped by the R.A.F. are released by Handley Page Hampden bombers into Danish coastal waters.

April 20 The training begins of air crews under the Empire Air Training Scheme, to be retitled later as the British Commonwealth Air Training Plan.

April 23 The British aircraft carriers H.M.S. *Ark Royal* and H.M.S. *Glorious* are despatched to give support off Andalsnes and Namsos to British, French and Norwegian forces resisting the German invaders in Norway.

April 24 Gloster Gladiators of No. 963 Squadron are flown off H.M.S. *Glorious* some 180 miles (290km) from shore, landing on the frozen Lake Lesjaskog near Andalsnes.

May 4 A Messerschmitt Bf 109E-3 of the Luftwaffe's II/JG 54, one of the first two just captured in France, is test flown at the Aircraft and Armament Experimental Establishment at Boscombe Down, England, allowing the first full evaluation of this front-line fighter by the Allies.

May 7 Aer Lingus operates its first service with a Douglas DC-3 (EI-ACA), on its Dublin–Liverpool route.

May 10 The German invasion of the Low Countries begins, preceded by extensive and effective deployment of paratroops and airborne troops. Belgium's 'impregnable' Fort Eban Emael is easily subjugated by the unexpected use of glider-borne assault troops. According to Luftwaffe records, its aircraft losses on the first day of the Belgium/Netherlands/France invasion are 304 destroyed and 51 damaged.

May 13 In the United States, the Sikorsky VS-300 single-rotor helicopter, which uses a small rotor at the tail to overcome the torque effect of the main rotor, makes its first free flight.

May 14 Germany threatens the destruction of all Dutch cities by aerial bombardment in surrender discussions at the Hague. The remainder of the world is shocked by the bombing of the business centre of Rotterdam by the Luftwaffe as these surrender negotiations are in progress. All bomber formations had been recalled when negotiations began but one group failed to receive radio instructions to abort the mission.

May 18 The British battleship H.M.S. *Resolution* is hit but not sunk by a 1,000-kg bomb from a Junkers Ju 88 near Narvik.

May 29 First flight of the Vought XF4U-1 prototype in the U.S. As the F4U Corsair, more than 12,000 are built to serve with the United States Navy and Marine Corps, and with America's Allies. Most air historians regard it as the best of the carrier-based fighters developed during the Second World War.

June 4 The British evacuation from the Dunkirk beaches is completed. More than 338,000 men are carried to Britain to fight again, this total including some 112,000 Belgians and French.

June 5 German forces regroup and begin the Battle of France. This proves to be an impressive demonstration of air power used in close-support of armour and infantry.

1940 Messerschmitt Bf 109E-3

June 8 The British 27,560-ton aircraft carrier H.M.S. *Glorious*, returning from operations off Norway with the remnants of Nos. 46 and 263 Squadrons aboard, is sunk by the German battleships *Gneisenau* and *Scharnhorst*.

June 11 The Italian air force, the Regia Aeronautica, makes its first attack on Malta.

June 11/12 The R.A.F. reacts to the Italian declaration of war by sending a force of 36 Whitley bombers to attack the Fiat works at Turin.

June 14 Jersey Airways begins to evacuate its staff and equipment to the U.K. mainland by air with assistance from the R.A.F.'s No. 24 (Communications) Squadron.

June 17–18 The last serviceable aircraft of the British Expeditionary Force are flown from Nantes, France to R.A.F. Tangmere, Sussex.

June 21 Hitler meets French officials in a railway carriage in Compiègne Forest, where the Armistice of 1918 had been signed, to accept their capitulation. Hostilities between France and Germany officially end four days later.

July 1/2 The R.A.F. drops its first 2,000-lb bomb in an attack on the battleship *Scharnhorst* at Kiel.

July 3 Aircraft of the Fleet Air Arm take part in an attack on the French fleet at Oran. This is made in an attempt to ensure that the vessels do not fall into German hands.

July 7 The Spanish airline Iberia is reformed as the national airline, financed originally by the Spanish Government and Deutsche Luft-Hansa.

July 10 Date regarded generally as the opening phase of the Luftwaffe/ R.A.F. confrontation known as the Battle of Britain.

July 14 Air reconnaissance provides evidence of a build-up of barges and materials at cross-Channel ports, clearly intended for a German invasion of Britain.

July 16 Bombardier training begins in U.S.A.A.C. schools, initially at Lowry Field, Colorado.

August First flight of the DFS 194 research aircraft under full rocket power at Peenemünde, piloted by Heini Dittmar.

First flight of the Focke-Achgelis Fa 223 Drache transport helicopter. After prolonged trials, small numbers are built and become operational late in 1943. (q.v. also September, 1945)

The Soviet I-200 (MiG-1) fighter, designed by Artyom I. Mikoyan and Mikhail I. Gurevich, successfully passes its State Acceptance tests. Ordered into production, it becomes the first of the famous MiG series of fighters.

August 16 Flt. Lt. J.B. Nicholson, R.A.F., wins the only Victoria Cross awarded to a pilot of Fighter Command by remaining in his blazing Hurricane in order to destroy a German aircraft over Southampton before baling out.

August 17 P.O. William M.L. Fiske, first regular American pilot to serve with the R.A.F., dies from wounds received on the previous day.

August 19 First flight of the North American B-25 medium bomber prototype, subsequently built in large numbers for service with the U.S. and its allies.

August 24/25 First German bombs fall on central London.

August 25/26 To maintain the status quo, 43 aircraft of Bomber Command comprising Hampdens, Wellingtons and Whitleys, make the R.A.F.'s first attack of the war on Berlin.

August 28 First flight of the experimental Italian Caproni-Campini N-1 monoplane, powered by a turbine that is driven by a piston engine.

September 2 The U.S.A. transfers 50 U.S. First World War destroyers to the U.K. in exchange for air and naval bases at eight strategic points.

September 6 An invasion alert is given to forces in Britain when air reconnaissance shows that barge and material concentrations in Channel ports has reached a high level.

September 7 The Luftwaffe begins to make heavy bombing attacks on London.

September 17 With the failure of the Luftwaffe to eliminate the R.A.F., Hitler orders Operation *Sea Lion* (the invasion of Britain) to be postponed.

September 27 Germany, Italy and Japan conclude a pact, each pledging total aid to the others.

October The Luftwaffe Gruppe Rowehl special high-altitude reconnaissance unit is instructed to start photographic mapping of western Russia and the frontier districts.

October 8 It is announced in the U.K. that the R.A.F. is to form a so-called Eagle Squadron, a Fighter Command unit to consist of volunteer pilots from the U.S.A.

October 12 First flight is recorded of the Ilyushin Il-2 third prototype, this being of similar configuration to the production version. The Il-2 is the first and most famous of the Soviet *Shturmoviki* (ground attack) aircraft used throughout the Second World War, and built to the tune of more than 36,000.

October 18 It is announced in the House of Commons that because of Luftwaffe attacks, almost half a million children have been evacuated from London and that thousands are still leaving daily.

1940 Caproni-Campini N-1

October 26 The first flight is made of the North American NA-73 fighter prototype which had been designed to meet a British requirement for use in Europe. Better known as the P-51 Mustang, more than 15,000 are built and the extensively-produced P-51D/K versions (almost 8,000) are regarded as classic examples of Second World War fighter aircraft.

November 10 The first organized transatlantic ferry flights of U.S.-built aircraft begin.

November 11 Italy's Regia Aeronautica makes its one and only major air attack on the U.K.

In what is now an historic action, Fairey Swordfish torpedo-bombers of the Fleet Air Arm decimate the Italian Fleet in a night attack on Taranto harbour.

November 14/15 Guided by X-Gerät radio beams, nearly 300 Luftwaffe bombers cause major damage to the city of Coventry, Warwickshire.

November 15 Resulting from the U.S.A.'s gain of bases by its destroyer deal with the U.K., U.S. Navy aircraft begin operations from Bermuda.

November 25 The first de Havilland DH.98 Mosquito prototype (W4050) makes its first flight at Hatfield, England. Designed as a bomber aircraft that would be fast enough to dispense with defensive armament, it has a level speed of almost 400mph (644km/h). It is to see wide-scale service in a variety of roles.

First flight of the Martin B-26 Marauder prototype (40-1361), a medium-range bomber to be used widely by the U.S.A.A.F.

November 29 A Lockheed Hudson, on delivery flight from the U.S.A., completes the first transatlantic ferry flight to terminate with a landing at Prestwick.

December First flight of the Yokosuka D4Y1 Suisei naval dive bomber, subsequently allocated the Allied SW Pacific reporting name 'Judy'.

December 18 In Germany, the first successful flight is made by a Henschel Hs 293A radio-controlled bomb.

First recorded flight of the Curtiss XSB2C-1 Helldiver prototype, a carrier-based scout-bomber which is to see service on U.S. Navy carriers in the Pacific theatre.

1941

January First flight of the Kawanishi H8K1 long-range flying-boat. Considered by many air historians to be one of the outstanding water-based aircraft of the Second World War, it is later allocated the Allied SW Pacific reporting name 'Emily'.

January 9 First flight of the Avro Lancaster prototype (BT308), then known as the Manchester III. It was, in fact, a converted Manchester airframe but powered by four Rolls-Royce Merlins. The production Lancaster becomes the best-known and most successful of the R.A.F.'s wartime heavy bombers.

January 16 Grand Harbour at Malta is bombed by Axis aircraft, H.M.S. *Illustrious* being damaged.

January 29 Luftwaffe aircraft air-drop mines into the Suez Canal.

February 25 First flight of the Me 321 *Gigant* large-capacity glider, designed for the airborne invasion of Britain which was later indefinitely postponed.

February 10 British paratroops, dropped by Whitley Vs of the R.A.F.'s Nos. 51 and 78 Squadrons, carry out the first British airborne operation of the Second World War, an unsuccessful attack on a viaduct at Tragino, Campagna, Italy.

February 10/11 The R.A.F.'s No. 7 Squadron, its first unit to fly four-engined bombers since the First World War, uses Stirlings operationally for the first time in an attack on Rotterdam.

February 24/25 First operational use of the Avro Manchester is made by the R.A.F. in an attack on targets at Brest, France.

March 10/11 First operational use by the R.A.F. of the Handley Page Halifax bomber, deployed against targets at Le Havre, France.

March 11 The Lend-Lease Act is authorized by President Roosevelt, allowing the supply of goods and services to nations that are considered vital to the defence of the U.S.A.

March 28 It is announced in the U.K. that the R.A.F.'s Eagle Squadron, composed of volunteer pilots from the U.S.A., is fully operational.

March 30/31 In the first of many attacks, 109 R.A.F. bombers are deployed against the German battleships *Gneisenau* and *Scharnhorst* at Brest, France.

April 1 In an attack on Emden, a Wellington of the R.A.F.'s No.149 Squadron drops the first 4,000-lb 'block-buster' bomb to be used operationally.

April 2 First flight of the Heinkel He 280V-1 prototype, the first aircraft to be designed as a jet fighter and also the first with twin-engined turbojet power plant.

April 9 An agreement is concluded between the United States and the Danish Government in exile, allowing the U.S. to build and operate airfields in Greenland.

April 15 Demonstrating his VS-300 at Stratford, Connecticut, Igor Sikorsky makes an officially recorded flight of 1 hr 5 mins 14.5 secs duration.

April 18 First flight of the Messerschmitt Me 262V-1 (PC-UA), powered by a single piston-engine because its intended turbojet engines have not materialized.

May First Soviet RUS-1 and RUS-2 air defence radar sets are put into service.

First flight of the Nakajima JINI Gekko twin-engined fighter. Modified to a night fighting role as the J1N1-S in 1943, it becomes the first Japanese aircraft to carry primitive AI radar and oblique-firing armament.

May 4 First operation on the North Atlantic Return Ferry Service is flown by Capt. D.C.T. Bennett, in a Consolidated Liberator I (AM258) from Montreal to Squires Gate, Blackpool.

May 6 First flight of the Republic XP-47B prototype (40-3051) designed by a team under the leadership of Alexander Kartveli. It is to be developed as the excellent Thunderbolt, built to more than 15,000 examples. It becomes one of the three outstanding U.S.A.A.F. fighters of the Second World War.

The Luftwaffe attacks several U.K. midland towns, claiming that the Rolls-Royce factory has been destroyed. Fortunately for the U.K., the attack has been diverted into open country by use of a 'beam bending' technique.

May 10/11 Rudolf Hess, Deputy Führer of Germany, flies to Britain in a Messerschmitt Bf 110 and lands by parachute in Scotland.

May 13–14 First mass flight of bomber aircraft over the Pacific, when the U.S.A.A.C. deploys 21 B-17s from Hamilton Field, California, to Hickham Field, Hawaii.

May 15 The first flight is made at R.A.F. Cranwell of the Gloster E.28/39 experimental jet-powered aircraft (W4041), piloted by P.E.G. Sayer. It is the first flight of a British turbojet-powered aircraft.

May 20 Operation *Mercury*, the largest airborne assault mounted by the Luftwaffe during the Second World War, lands 22,750 men on the island of Crete. A successful operation, it results in seizure of the island, but losses of about 5,600 men and some 150 transport aircraft bring an end to Luftwaffe paratroop operations.

May 26 A Catalina of the R.A.F.'s No. 209 Squadron spots the 50,150-ton German battleship *Bismarck* in the Atlantic. Its steering gear is subsequently damaged in an attack by Swordfish from H.M.S. *Ark Royal*, enabling her to be sunk by British warships.

First flight of the Japanese Kayaba Ka-1 artillery observation autogyro. Converted to an anti-submarine role carrying light bombs, the Ka-1 later becomes the first armed rotary wing aircraft used in action.

June 20 The United States Army Air Force is formed, with Major Gen. H.H. Arnold as its chief.

June 22 Operation *Barbarossa*, the German invasion of the Soviet Union, begins with a massive surprise air strike. By nightfall, Soviet losses amount to 1,811 aircraft (1,489 destroyed on the ground for the loss of only 35 Luftwaffe aircraft), but this success is never repeated.

At 043 hrs, Lt. Kokorev of the 124th Fighter Rgt. Red Air Force, deliberately rams a Luftwaffe Bf 110 – the first instance of a taran (battering ram) attack during this war.

July 8 The R.A.F. makes a daylight attack on Wilhelmshaven using Fortress Is received from the U.S.; this represents the first operational use of the Boeing B-17 Flying Fortress.

July 18 The formation of R.A.F. Ferry Command is announced.

July 21/22 Luftwaffe bombers make their first night attack on Moscow.

August 1 First operational use of Soviet 'parasite' I-16SPB high-speed dive bombers (variant of the standard fighter) carried under the wings of TB-3 heavy bombers. These make a successful attack on Constanta, Romania. (q.v. December 3, 1931)

The U.S. bans the export of aviation fuel, except to the U.K. and unoccupied nations resisting the Nazis. This comes as a severe blow to the Japanese, involved in a continuing war with China, and hastens a decision to unite with its Axis partners in war against the Allies.

First flight of the German XTBF-1 Avenger prototype destined to become the U.S. Navy's standard torpedo-bomber of the Second World War.

August 3 To provide interim air cover for North Atlantic convoys, the U.K. develops a 'Catafighter' scheme. The first success is gained on this date when a Sea Hurricane, catapulted from H.M.S. *Maplin*, destroys a German Focke-Wulf Fw 200 Condor on maritime patrol.

August 7/8 A small number of Soviet DB-3F bombers of the Soviet Naval Aviation take off from the Estonian islands of Dagö and Saaremaa and raid the Berlin area, which is brightly lit. From then on, Berlin is under strict blackout regulations.

August 13 First flight of the Me 163A prototype under full rocket power at Peenemünde.

August 18 President Roosevelt announces that Pan American Airways is to ferry U.S.-built warplanes to British forces in the Middle East.

August 27 Following determined attacks by a Lockheed Hudson of the R.A.F.'s No. 269 Squadron patrol in the North Atlantic, the German submarine U-570 surrenders to the Hudson. This is the first U-boat to be captured by the R.A.F.

September 7 Hawker Hurricane I fighters of Nos. 81 and 134 Squadrons fly off H.M.S. *Argus* to land on a Soviet airfield near Murmansk, to help bolster the local defences. The aircraft were later handed to the Soviet air force.

September 14 Messerschmitt Me 321 giant assault transport gliders of Staffel [G-S] 1 are first used operationally during the airborne attack on the Saaremaa island in the Baltic, as part of an attempt to capture the fort at Kübassaare.

September 16 Following an attack of the previous week, the Luftwaffe drops leaflets on Leningrad, threatening its immediate destruction if the city does not surrender.

September 23 Oberleutnant Hans-Urich Rudel, flying a Ju 87, succeeds in hitting the 26,170-ton Soviet battleship *Marat* at Kronshtadt with a 2,205-lb (1,000kg) bomb. The ship is badly damaged and sinks in shallow water. This is almost certainly the greatest single success achieved by a dive bomber pilot in the Second World War.

September 24 BOAC carries out its first operation on the North Atlantic Return Ferry service, using Liberator Is provided by R.A.F. Ferry Command.

September 30 To date, the Luftwaffe claims to have destroyed more than 4,500 Soviet aircraft since the beginning of the invasion.

October First flight of the Heinkel He IIIZ, a five-engined heavy glider tug specifically designed to tow the Me 321. It unites two He IIIH fuselages by a constant-chord wing section mounting the fifth engine.

October 2 The third Me 163A rocket-powered prototype, piloted by Heini Dittmar, achieves a speed of 623.85mph (1,004km/h), an unofficial world speed record that remains secret until the end of hostilities.

October 12 BOAC begins a U.K. to Cairo service, the first flight operated by C-class flying-boat *Clare* (G-AFCZ) routed via Lisbon, Gibraltar and Malta.

October 30 A Consolidated B-24 Liberator with Maj. Alva L. Harvey in command completes a round-the-world flight carrying personnel of the Harriman Mission.

October 31 It is announced that R.A.F. aircraft operating from Malta have destroyed some 76,500 tons of enemy shipping in the Mediterranean.

1941 Wrecked aircraft at Pearl Harbor (courtesy U.S. Navy Photographic Center)

November 12 The British aircraft carrier H.M.S. *Ark Royal* is sunk by the German submarine U-81 off Gibraltar.

November 30 First Whitleys to be equipped with ASV Mk 11 long-range radar are those operated by the R.A.F.'s No. 502 Squadron. On this date, a Whitley VII (Z9190) of the squadron scores Coastal Command's first ASV destruction of an enemy submarine, the U-206, in the Bay of Biscay.

December First flight of the Kawasaki Ki-61 'Hien' fighter prototype. Allocated the Allied SW Pacific reporting name of 'Tony', it is the only Japanese fighter powered by a liquid-cooled engine to see operational service during the Second World War.

First flight of the Soviet Lavochkin La-5 fighter prototype, radial-engined development of the LaGG-3. La-5 fighters first became operational near Stalingrad in September, 1942. (q.v. March 30, 1940)

December 1 The U.S. Civil Air Patrol is established, formed to utilize American civil pilots and their aircraft for wartime duties.

December 7 Using carrier-based aircraft, and without any declaration of war, the Japanese attack Pearl Harbor, Hawaii, causing extensive damage to the U.S. Pacific Fleet and shore installations.

December 8 Following intensive air attacks on R.A.F. bases in Malaya and Singapore, the Japanese invade northern Malaya.

Lockheed Hudsons are used by the Royal Australian Air Force in its first attacks of the Second World War, made against Japanese forces invading Pacific islands.

December 10 U.S.A.A.F. B-17 Flying Fortress bombers make the first American air offensive of the year attacking Japanese shipping.

Aircraft from the U.S.S. *Enterprise* record the first U.S. victory of the war against a Japanese combat ship, sinking a submarine north of the Hawaiian Islands.

The British battleships H.M.S. *Prince of Wales* and H.M.S. *Impulse* are sunk by Japanese Mitsubishi G3M 'Nell' bombers.

December 18 Lt. 'Buzz' Wagner of the U.S.A.A.F. becomes the first American 'ace' of the Second World War, destroying his fifth Japanese aircraft over the Philippines.

December 21/22 An ASV-equipped Fairey Swordfish of the FAA's No. 812 Squadron sinks the first German U-boat (U-451) to be destroyed by an aircraft at night.

1942

January–May German troops cut off by Soviet forces at Kholm are supplied by air by using DFS 230 and Go 242 cargo gliders, the first large-scale use of air supply to own forces behind enemy lines.

January 1 Following the signature of the United Nations Declaration on this date, the name United Nations is adopted by the coalition of powers fighting the Axis. The name is perpetuated in the United Nations Organization.

January 14 The first flight is made at Stratford, Connecticut of the Sikorsky XR-4 helicopter prototype (41-18874). (q.v. October 30, 1943)

January 28 Two of the earliest North American Mustang Is used by the R.A.F. (AG360 and AG365) are sent to the Air Development Fighting Unit at Duxford. The first operational squadron to receive them is No. 26, in February 1942, with the first operational sortie flown over France on May 5, 1942.

February 1 First carrier offensive made by the U.S.S. *Enterprise* and U.S.S. *Yorktown*, their aircraft attacking enemy installations on several of the Marshall and Gilbert Islands.

February 8–9 Following heavy air bombardment, Japanese forces land on Singapore, capturing Tengah airfield.

February 10 The last R.A.F. fighters are withdrawn from Singapore to bases in Sumatra.

February 12 The German warships *Gneisenau*, *Scharnhorst* and *Prinz Eugen*, protected by a strong defensive air cover of fighters, escape through the English Channel.

February 19 A first practical demonstration of Australia's vulnerability is made clear when Japanese bombers attack shipping in harbour at Port Darwin, Australia.

February 22 The first U.S.A.A.F. Headquarters in Europe is established in the U.K. under the command of Brigadier-Gen. I.C. Eaker.

Air Marshal Arthur Harris is appointed Commander-in-Chief, R.A.F. Bomber Command.

February 27 The U.K. Army Air Corps is formed, comprising the Glider Pilot Regiment, the Airborne Infantry Units and the Parachute Regiment.

February 27–28 A first British combined operation against Europe, and involving air, land and sea forces, is made against Bruneval in northern France. After overcoming German resistance, components are removed from a Würzburg ground radar station which is then destroyed before the forces withdraw.

March First flight of the Focke-Achgelis Fa 330 Bachstelze submarine-borne rotor kite. It becomes operational in summer 1942, but is never very popular with the submarine crews due to the delays in submerging when attacked.

First flight of the Messerschmitt Me 323 *Gigant* six-engined large-capacity transport, a powered version of the Me 321 glider.

March 3 The R.A.F.'s No. 44 Squadron makes the first operational sortie with its new Avro Lancaster bombers, a mine-laying operation in the Heligoland Bight.

March 20 First flight of the Mitsubishi J2MI Raiden naval fighter prototype at Kasumiga-ura. It was subsequently allocated the Allied SW Pacific reporting name of 'Jack'.

1942 Messerschmitt Me 323 Gigant

1942 During the Grumman Avenger's operational debut during the Battle of Midway on June 4, only one of the six newly-arrived aircraft survive an attack on Japanese ships

March 25 Unsuccessful flight test of the first Me 262 V1 prototype powered by two early BMW 003 turbojets and a central Jumo 210G piston engine.

April 2 The U.S. Tenth Army Air Force makes its first combat operation, heavy bombers attacking shipping off the Andaman Islands.

April 2–9 Japanese carrier-based aircraft operating off the coasts of Ceylon and India cause considerable damage to installations at Colombo and Trincomalee. Royal Navy operations to intercept the enemy fleet are disastrous, the aircraft carrier H.M.S. *Hermes*, the cruisers H.M.S. *Cornwall* and *Devonshire* and the destroyer *Vampire* all being sunk by carrier-based aircraft.

April 6 Carrier-based aircraft from the Japanese formation mentioned above are the first to make air attacks against India.

April 12 Three U.S.A.A.F. B-17s and ten B-25s based in Australia make the first attack against Japanese shipping and installations in the Philippines.

April 18 In a one-way attack on Tokyo, 16 B-25s led by Lt. Col. J.H. Doolittle are flown off the carrier U.S.S. *Hornet* some 400 miles (640km) at sea. Having completed the attack, most of the aircraft force-land in China.

April 19 First night of the Macchi C.205 fighter prototype, arguably the best Italian fighter of the Second World War.

April 20 Malta's air defence is reinforced by 47 Spitfires flown off the U.S.S. *Wasp* about 660 miles (1062km) west of the island.

April 22 The Assam, Burma, China Ferry Command is established to air-ferry supplies to China over the Himalayas ('Hump route').

April 26 Winston Churchill instructs the U.K. Petroleum Warfare Department to investigate ways of dispersing fog from emergency airfields.

May 7–8 The Battle of the Coral Sea is fought by carrier-based aircraft of opposing Japanese and U.S. fleets. It was the first vital naval battle to be fought without a surface ship of either side sighting the enemy fleet. The U.S. Navy loses U.S.S. *Lexington* and 69 aircraft. The Japanese lose *Shoho* and 85 aircraft and *Shokaku* is damaged, which prevents its use during the Battle of Midway.

May 10 The U.S. carrier U.S.S. *Ranger*, off the African Gold Coast, flies off 60 U.S.A.A.F. Curtiss P-40s to Accra. They were then flown in stages to join with the U.S. Tenth Army Air Force in India.

May 26 The first flight is made by the Northrop XP-61 prototype. The U.S.A.A.F.'s first purpose-designed radar-equipped night fighter, the P-61 Black Widow enters operational use in the Pacific theatre in 1944.

May 30/31 R.A.F. Bomber Command mounts its first 'thousand bomber' raid against a German target. Deployed against Cologne, 1,046 aircraft are involved, 599 of them being Vickers Wellingtons.

May 31 The R.A.F. uses de Havilland Mosquitos operationally for the first time in a daylight follow-up attack on Cologne by aircraft of No. 105 Squadron.

June 3/4 A Vickers Wellington of the R.A.F.'s No. 172 Squadron is the first to make a night attack on an enemy submarine by using a Leigh light to illuminate its target.

June 3–4 The Battle of Midway is fought, one of the decisive battles of history in which the Japanese aircraft carriers *Akagi*, *Hiryu*, *Kaga* and *Soryu* are destroyed by carrier-based aircraft of the U.S. Navy (the cruiser *Mikuma* is also lost). The Japanese Navy, deprived of its in-being carrier force, had lost the initiative and from that moment forward is compelled to fight the defensive. The U.S. Navy loses the original U.S.S. *Yorktown* and the destroyer U.S.S. *Hammann*.

June 12 Twelve U.S.A.A.F. B-24 Liberators make an unsuccessful strike against the Ploesti oil refineries. It is the U.S.A.A.F.'s first attack against a strategic target in the Balkans.

June 13 The German A4 (V2) rocket is launched for the first time at Peenemünde, but quickly goes out of control and crashes.

June 18 Major Gen. Carl Spaatz is appointed to command the U.S. Eighth Army Air Force in the U.K.

June 26 First flight of the Grumman XF6F-3 Hellcat prototype (02982), a significant Allied shipboard fighter of the Second World War.

July 1 A Boeing B-17 Flying Fortress, the first aircraft to begin equipping the U.S. Eighth Army Air Force in the U.K., lands at Prestwick.

1942 Douglas Devastators of VT-8 from U.S.S. Hornet *attack* Kaga *during the Battle of Midway. Led by Lt. Cmdr. John Waldron, all 15 unescorted aircraft were lost in an heroic attack (courtesy U.S. Navy Photographic Center)*

July 4 Six crews of the U.S. 15th Bombardment Squadron make the first U.S.A.A.F. bomber mission over Europe in the Second World War. Flying R.A.F. Douglas Bostons, they make attacks on four enemy-held airfields in Holland.

July 18 A first jet-powered flight is made by the Messerschmitt Me 262V-3 prototype (PC-UC), fitted with two Junkers 109-004A turbojets, each developing 1,852lb (840kg). The pilot is Fritz Wendel.

August 15 The R.A.F.'s Pathfinder Force is formed under the command of Air Commodore D.C.T. Bennett.

August 16/17 The first exploratory use of the Pathfinder Force is made in an attack on Emden, Germany.

August 17 The U.S.A.A.F. makes its first Second World War heavy bomber attack against targets in Western Europe. B-17s of the 97th Bombardment Group attack the Rouen-Scotteville marshalling yards in occupied France.

August 20 The U.S. Twelfth Army Air Force is activated at Bolling Field, Washington D.C., in preparation for the invasion of North Africa.

August 24 The first Junkers Ju 86P-2 very high altitude pressurized reconnaissance aircraft is intercepted and destroyed. This is achieved by an R.A.F. Spitfire VC from Alexandria, making its interception at about 42,000ft (12,800m) although the pilot had no pressurized protection against operation at that height.

September A Yokosuka E14Y1 ('Glen') light submarine-borne reconnaissance floatplane, launched from the Japanese submarine I-25, makes two overflights of the wooded Oregon coast and drops four incendiary bombs. It is the first and only time Japanese fixed-wing aircraft raid the U.S.A. during the Second World War.

September 1 R.A.F. and U.S. Navy Catalinas disperse a 'wolf pack' of German submarines attacking a west-bound North Atlantic convoy. One of the submarines is sunk.

September 2 A first flight is made by the Hawker Tempest prototype (HM595), a Mk V built as a conversion of a Hawker Typhoon.

September 12 The first use of para-fragmentation bombs in the Second World War is made by the U.S.A.A.F.'s 89th Attack Squadron during sweeps over Buna airstrip, New Guinea.

September 16 Shortly after the third anniversary of the formation of the U.K.'s Air Transport Auxiliary, it is announced that its pilots had ferried some 100,000 aircraft of 117 different types.

September 21 First flight of the Boeing B-29 Superfortress prototype (41-2) is made at Seattle, Washington.

September 23 Brigadier Gen. J.H. Doolittle is appointed commander of the U.S.A.A.F.'s new Twelfth Air Force.

September 25 A low-level attack on the Gestapo headquarters in Oslo, Norway, is made by Mosquito bombers of the R.A.F.'s No. 105 Squadron.

September 29 The Eagle Squadrons serving with the R.A.F. are formally taken over by the U.S.A.A.F.'s VIIIth Fighter Command and integrated with its 4th Fighter Group.

October 1 The first flight of a Bell XP-59A Airacomet prototype, the first turbojet-powered aircraft to fly in the United States.

October 3 The first fully successful launch of a German A4 (V2) ballistic rocket is made at Peenemünde.

October 21 Using B-24 Liberators, the U.S.A.A.F.'s India Air Task Force makes its first attack north of the Yellow River, China.

The U.S.A.A.F.'s VIIIth Bomber Command flies its first operation, attacking German submarine bases in occupied France.

October 21–22 BOAC makes an experimental flight from Prestwick to Ramenskoye, near Moscow. The non-stop flight of 13 hrs 9 mins is made in a converted Liberator 1.

October 25 In a first attack on Japanese-occupied Hong Kong, U.S. bomber aircraft cause damage to Kowloon docks.

November 2 The Patuxent River Naval Air Station is established by the U.S. Navy as a test unit for aircraft, equipment and materials.

November 8–11 U.S.A.A.F. aircraft operating from offshore U.S. Navy aircraft carriers contribute air cover for the Allied invasion of North Africa under Operation *Torch*.

November 9–10 To counter the Allied invasion, large numbers of Luftwaffe fighters and bomber aircraft are flown into Tunis and troop reinforcements are brought in by air and sea.

November 12 The U.S. Ninth Army Air Force is established in the Middle East.

November 15 First flight of the Heinkel He 219 twin-engined night fighter prototype. Operational from June 1943, it is the Luftwaffe's first operational aircraft with retractable tricycle landing gear and the first in the world with crew ejection seats.

November 25 Start of Luftwaffe supply flights into Stalingrad. The last remaining landing field at Tatsinskaya is lost to Soviet tanks on December 24.

November 28 The U.S.A.A.F.'s 7th Bomb Group makes a first attack on Bangkok, capital of Japanese-held Thailand, involving a 2,760-mile (4,440-km) round trip from Gaya, India.

1942 Two evaluation Bell YP-59A Airacomets

December 4 Making the U.S.A.A.F.'s first attack on Italy, B-24 Liberators of the Ninth Air Force bomb Naples.

December 20/21 Japanese bombers make the first night attack on Calcutta, India.

Mosquito bombers of the R.A.F.'s No. 109 Squadron, equipped with Oboe radar, are used in a night Pathfinder operation for the first time.

December 22 Consolidated B-24 Liberators of the U.S.A.A.F.'s 307th Bombardment Group make the first major air attack on a Japanese air base in the Central Pacific.

December 23 The U.K. Government sets up a committee under the chairmanship of Lord Brabazon of Tara to make recommendations on suitable civil transport aircraft for early post-war development.

December 27 First flight of the Kawanishi N1KI-J Shiden naval fighter prototype, allocated the Allied SW Pacific reporting name of 'George'.

1943

January 5 The U.S.A.A.F.'s Northwest African Air Forces are activated with Major Gen. Carl Spaatz in command.

January 9 The first flight is recorded of the first Lockheed Model L-49 Constellation at Burbank, California. Commandeered on the production line for service with the U.S.A.A.F. under the designation C-69, it is still bearing its civil registration NX67900.

January 14–23 In a conference at Casablanca, Morocco, Churchill, Roosevelt and their chiefs-of-staff reach some important decisions: to step up round-the-clock bombing of targets in Germany, to begin an invasion of Europe's 'soft underbelly' with Sicily as the initial objective, and to defer the cross-Channel invasion until 1944.

January 27 Attacking Emden and Wilhelmshaven, B-17s of the 1st Bombardment Wing, Eighth Air Force, make the U.S.A.A.F.'s first heavy-bomber attack on Germany.

January 30 Mosquito bombers of the R.A.F.'s No.105 Squadron make the first daylight raid on Berlin.

February 11 Air Marshal Sir Arthur Tedder, R.A.F., is appointed to be Air C-in-C Mediterranean Air Command.

February 13 The first operational use is made of Vought F4U Corsair aircraft of Marine Fighter Squadron 124 escorting Navy PB4Y Liberators in an attack on Bougainville.

March 5 A first flight is made by the Gloster Meteor prototype (DG206). The Meteor becomes the first turbojet aircraft to enter service with the R.A.F. and the only Allied turbojet to see operational service during the Second World War.

March 10 The U.S. Fourteenth Army Air Force is activated, commanded by Major Gen. Claire Chennault.

March 24 Battle of the Bismarck Sea, during which a major Japanese attempt to reinforce Lae is foiled by aircraft of the

Southwest Pacific Air Forces. Some 40,000 tons of Japanese shipping is sunk and almost 60 enemy aircraft destroyed.

April 5 Operation *Flax* is initiated to make concentrated air attacks on German and Italian transport aircraft shuttling arms and reinforcements from Italy to Tunisia.

April 18 Massacre of German transport aircraft off Cape Bon, Tunisia. Claims of 52 aircraft destroyed are made by British and U.S. fighters.

Admiral Isoroku Yamamoto, Japan's protagonist of naval air power, is killed when the Mitsubishi G4M 'Betty' carrying him and his staff is ambushed and destroyed over Bougainville. This attack is made by Lockheed P-38G Lightnings of the U.S.A.A.F.'s 339th Fighter Squadron, flying 550 miles (885km) from their base to make the interception.

May 17/18 Historic attack by the R.A.F.'s No. 617 Squadron, led by Wing Cmdr. Guy Gibson, against the Ruhr dams. So-called 'bouncing bomb' mines are used, conceived by Barnes Wallis.

May 23 In a new demonstration of the versatility of the Fairey Swordfish, one operating from the escort carrier H.M.S. *Archer* sinks the German submarine U-572 by rocket attack.

June The Messerschmitt Me 262A jet-powered fighter is ordered into series production.

June 1 In advance of receiving its Boeing B-29 Superfortresses, the U.S.A.A.F.'s 58th Very Heavy Bombardment Wing is activated at Marietta, Georgia. It is created to make strategic attacks on Japanese targets.

June 11 The surrender of the Italian garrison on the island of Pantellaria, midway between Tunisia and Sicily, followed intensive bombing by Allied aircraft. It is the first occasion that a large defended area is conquered by air power alone.

June 15 The Arado Ar 234V-I Blitz (Lightning), the prototype of the world's first turbojet-powered recce-bomber, makes its first flight.

June 28 First mention is made that air reconnaissance of Peenemünde had revealed large rockets which might be intended for long-range attack.

July 9 Following a month-long bombardment of Axis air bases on Sicily, Sardinia and Italy, the British Eighth Army and U.S. Seventh Army invade Sicily. The amphibious landings are preceded with an assault by paratroops and a large number of troop and cargo-carrying gliders.

July 18 The U.S. Navy airship K-74 is shot down by a German submarine off the Florida coast. It was the only U.S. airship to be destroyed by enemy action during the Second World War.

July 22 The Canadian Government's transatlantic service for mail, military personnel and VIPs is inaugurated, being operated by Trans-Canada Air Lines.

July 24/25 The anti-radar device known as 'Window' is used by the R.A.F. for the first time during an attack on Hamburg.

July 30 First flight of the Arado Ar 234A jet reconnaissance bomber prototype.

August 1 U.S.A.A.F. Mediterranean-based B-24 Liberators make a low-level attack on the Ploesti oil refineries in Romania. This is the U.S.A.A.F.'s first low-level attack by heavy bombers against a strongly defended target, and its longest-range bombing mission to date.

August 2/3 R.A.F. Bomber Command makes its fourth major attack on Hamburg within ten days. More than 3,000 bombers are employed in these attacks, but thanks to the use of 'Window' the 87 aircraft which were lost represented 2.6 per cent of the total, rather than the more usual average of about 6 per cent for such operations.

August 17 In daylight attacks against Regensburg and Schweinfurt, the U.S. Eighth Army Air Force loses 59 heavy bombers.

August 17/18 R.A.F. bombers make a heavy attack on the German research establishment at Peenemünde, intended to destroy or delay the design and production of advanced weapons.

First operational use by the Luftwaffe of the Henschel HS 293A-1 rocket-powered remotely-controlled glide bomb, when Dornier Do217E-5s of II/KG 100 carry out an anti-shipping strike against British ships in the Bay of Biscay.

August 27 The British corvette H.M.S. *Egret*, on patrol in the Bay of Biscay, is sunk by an air-launched Henschel Hs 993 radio-controlled bomb.

August 31 First operational use of the Grumman F6F Hellcat by U.S. Navy squadron VF-5 flown off the carrier U.S.S. *Yorktown* in an attack by Navy Task Force 15 against Japanese positions on Marcus Island.

September First flight of the DFS 228 rocket-powered high-altitude reconnaissance aircraft prototype in glider form, released from a Do 217K carrier.

September 3 Peace negotiations between the Allies and Italy are concluded in secret. The armistice became effective on September 8.

September 9 The Italian 46,200-ton battleship *Roma* is sunk by two Ruhrstahl/Kramer Fritz X-1 radio-controlled bombs air-launched by Luftwaffe Dornier Do. 217s.

September 12 Benito Mussolini, being held prisoner at an hotel in the Gran Sasso mountains, is rescued by German glider troops and airlifted to safety in a Fieseler Fi 156 Storch.

September 13 In attempts to enable the Allies to break out from the beachhead at Salerno, a reinforcing 1,200 paratroopers of the U.S. 82nd Airborne Division are airdropped.

September 15/16 An R.A.F. Lancaster makes the first operational use of a 12,000-lb bomb, this being dropped on the Dortmund-Ems canal in Germany.

September 20 The prototype of the de Havilland Vampire turbojet-powered single-seat fighter (LZ548) makes its first flight at Hatfield, Hertfordshire.

October 14 In a second major attack on ball bearing factories at Schweinfurt, the U.S.A.A.F. loses 60 out of 288 bombers despatched on the mission. Following this attack, the German ball bearing industry is dispersed.

October 16 The U.S. Ninth Army Air Force is reorganized in the U.K. to serve as a tactical arm of the U.S.A.A.F.

October 26 First flight of the Dornier Do 335 single-seat multi-role fighter prototype (CP+UA), powered by both tractor and pusher engines.

October 30 In order to evaluate the capability of the helicopter, the U.S. Navy acquires a single Sikorsky YR-4B from the U.S.A.A.F. (46445), redesignating it HMS-1.

October 31 The U.S. Navy scores its first aerial victory by the use of airborne interception radar when an AI-equipped Vought F4U-2 Corsair destroys a Japanese aircraft in New Guinea.

November 2 First operation of the newly-formed U.S. Fifteenth Army Air Force is an attack by 112 heavy bombers on aircraft factories at Wiener Neustadt, Austria.

November 5 Carrier-based aircraft from U.S.S. *Princeton* and U.S.S. *Saratoga* seriously damage Japanese cruisers and destroyers steaming from Truk through Rabaul.

November 11 Further severe damage is caused to Japanese naval vessels off Rabaul by aircraft from the U.S. Navy carriers *Bunker Hill*, *Essex* and *Independence*.

Aircraft of the U.S. Fifth and Thirteenth Army Air Forces co-operating with U.S. Navy carrier-based aircraft launch a major attack on Rabaul.

November 25 A force of Lockheed P-38s, North American B-25s and P-51s of the U.S. Fourteenth Army Air Force make a first attack on Formosa from bases in China.

November 27 The U.S.A.A.F.'s 20th Bomber Command is activated at Smoky Hill Army Air Field, Salina, Kansas.

November 30 The U.S. Navy's giant Martin Mars flying-boat makes a first operational non-stop flight of 4,375 miles (7,040km) from its Patuxent River base to Natal, Brazil.

December 13 Marking the beginning of long-range operations with fighter escort, the U.S.A.A.F.'s 8th and 9th Air Forces eventually fly 1,462 daylight sorties.

December 17 Orville Wright, on the 40th anniversary of making his first powered flight, presents the Collier Trophy for outstanding achievement in aviation to his former pupil Gen. H.H. ('Hap') Arnold.

December 20 Allied aircraft begin intensive bombing attacks on V-1 launching sites that are being prepared in Northern France. It causes the Germans to change over to quick-assembly prefabricated sites.

1944

Dr. Ing. Theodor von Kármán takes the post of chairman to the Scientific Advisory Board, U.S.A.A.F. (He initiated the first U.S. Army rocket motor project while holding positions at the California Institute of Technology during 1926–49.)

January 1 The United States Strategic Air Forces in Europe (U.S.S.A.F.E.) is activated.

January 4 The first high-altitude mine-dropping operation is made by an R.A.F. Halifax bomber off Brest, France.

January 9 First flight of the Lockheed XP-80 Shooting Star prototype (44-83020) is made at Muroc Dry Lake, California. It becomes, in December 1945, the first single-seat turbojet-powered fighter/fighter-bomber to enter service with the U.S.A.A.F. in P-80A form.

January 18 U.S. Navy Catalinas equipped with magnetic anomaly detection (MAD) equipment begin to patrol the Straits of Gibraltar. This is intended to prevent German submarines from getting into the Mediterranean.

January 22 Large-scale Allied landings, protected by massive air support, put some 50,000 Anglo-American troops ashore at Anzio, Italy without opposition.

February 15 Several hundred Allied medium/heavy bombers attack the monastery of Monte Cassino, Italy, ahead of the advancing American 5th Army.

February 17 A massive air attack is made against German formations endeavouring to push the Allied forces off the Anzio beachhead.

Twelve radar-equipped Grumman TBF-1C Avengers of the U.S. Navy, operating from the U.S.S. *Enterprise*, attack Truk by night. This was the first night bombing attack to be made from a U.S. aircraft carrier.

February 18 Mosquito bombers make a daring low-level daylight attack on the German prison at Amiens, France, attempting to liberate patriots awaiting execution for aiding the Allies.

February 29 Aircraft of the U.S. Fifth Army Air Force support the first landing made on the Admiralty Islands, thus completing the isolation of Rabaul.

March 4 First U.S.A.A.F. bombing raid on Berlin, undertaken by Boeing B-17G Flying Fortresses of the 8th Air Force.

March 5 Brigadier Gen. Orde Wingate's special force lands at 'Broadway', North Burma, in a night glider operation.

March 6 In its first major attack on Berlin, the U.S.A.A.F. deploys a force of 660 heavy bombers. A total of 69 bombers and 11 escort fighters are lost.

March 25 In landing aboard H.M.S. *Indefatigable*, the pre-prototype of the de Havilland Sea Mosquito (LR359) becomes the first British twin-engined aircraft to land on the deck of an aircraft carrier.

First operational use by the U.S. 15th Air Force of the VB-I Azon bomb, a general-purpose bomb with a pair of radio-controlled rudders in the tail.

April The Rolls-Royce Derwent I begins flight tests in a Gloster Meteor flying test bed.

April 4 The U.S. Twentieth Army Air Force is activated in Washington, D.C.

May 1 Allied aircraft begin a major offensive against the rail transport system of Western Europe.

May 10 Completion of the Chengtu Project, the construction of bomber and fighter airfields in China. This has been accomplished by some 400,000 Chinese coolies using primitive equipment.

June 1 The U.S. Navy records a first Atlantic crossing by non-rigid airships, from South Weymouth, Massachusetts to Port Lautey, Morocco, via Argentina and the Azores.

June 3 A Luftwaffe Junkers Ju 290A transport lands in Greenland to evacuate 26 men of the Bassgeiger weather station, who had been there for ten months.

June 6 Preceded by airdrops, the D-Day landings on the Normandy coast begin. The biggest amphibious assault in history, it is supported by massive Allied air force operations involving almost 5,000 sorties. By nightfall some five divisions are established ashore.

June 7 The first Allied airstrip to be completed in Normandy following the D-Day landings becomes operational at Asnelles, northeast of Bayeux.

June 11 U.S. Navy Task Force 58, comprising seven heavy and eight light aircraft carriers, is assembled and begins to deploy its aircraft in the opening of the campaign to occupy the Mariana Islands.

June 13 The first German V1 flying bombs are launched from sites in France against British targets.

June 15 With massive air support from the Task Force carriers, U.S. forces begin making landings on Saipan, Mariana Islands.

Boeing B-29 Superfortresses of the U.S.A.A.F.'s 20th Bomber Command make a first attack on Japan, deployed from their new bases in Chengtu, China.

June 15-16 With growing experience, German launching crews begin to step up the number of VI flying bombs being despatched against targets in England.

June 24/25 First use by the Luftwaffe of its Mistel composite. The initial variant comprises an upper piloted Messerschmitt Bf 109F-4, mounted above a Ju 88A-4 carrying a warhead containing 3,803lb (1,725kg) of high explosive. In this initial night operation, five composites are deployed against Allied shipping in the Seine Bay. (q.v. March 9, 1945)

June 25 Some 2,400 Allied bomber aircraft make a three-hour saturation raid on German positions forward of the American lines at St.-Lô, France.

July 5 A first powered flight is recorded by the Northrop MX-324, the first American rocket-powered military aircraft.

July 12 The first two operational Gloster Meteors are delivered to the R.A.F.'s No. 616 Squadron, then based at Culmhead, Somerset.

July 17 The first operational use of napalm incendiary material is made by U.S.A.A.F. P-38 Lightnings during attacks on a fuel depot at Coutances, France.

July 20 First operational use of the Arado Ar 234A turbojet-powered reconnaissance aircraft, flying from Juvincourt, near Reims.

July 27 Gloster Meteors are used operationally for the first time in attacks on VIs. These are unsuccessful because of gun-firing problems.

July 28 First flight of the de Havilland Hornet prototype (RR915). These single-seat long-range fighter/fighter-bombers, which enter service with the R.A.F. after the war, prove to be the fastest twin piston-engined combat aircraft in the world.

July 29 A battle-damaged B-29 of the U.S.A.A.F.'s 20th Bomber Command lands near Vladivostok and is immediately seized by the Soviet authorities. This B-29 is followed by another three on August 20, November 11 and November 21, 1944. These B-29s are carefully dismantled, examined and serve as pattern aircraft for the Tupolev Tu-4, the first modern Soviet heavy long-range bomber. (q.v. August 3, 1947)

August 2 The First Allied Airborne Army is formed under the command of Lt. Gen. Lewis H. Brereton, U.S.A.A.F.

August 4 Destroying a V1, by flying alongside it and using the wing of his Gloster Meteor to tip the missile and force it to the ground, Flt. Off. Dean of No. 616 Squadron scores the Meteor's first combat success.

In a first mission codenamed *Aphrodite*, radio-controlled B-17s, each packed with 20,000lb (9,072kg) of TNT, are launched against German V2 sites being constructed at Pas de Calais, France.

August 7 The U.S. Navy Carrier Division 11 is commissioned. Comprising the aircraft carriers U.S.S. *Ranger* and U.S.S.

1944 Lockheed P-80A Shooting Stars

1944 U.S.A.A.F. 8th Air Force Boeing B-17Gs (courtesy U.S. Air Force)

1944 Messerschmitt Me 163B-1 Komet (courtesy DaimlerChrysler Aerospace)

Saratoga, it is the first division intended specifically for night operations.

August 8/9 The Mediterranean Air Forces drop arms and supplies to the Polish Home Army in Warsaw that has been uprising against German forces since August 1. This is the first of several such operations.

August 14/15 Mediterranean Allied Air Forces fly more than 4,000 sorties and transport more than 9,000 airborne troops to begin the invasion of southern France, between Cannes and Hyères. The paratroops are dropped at night and in thick fog.

August 16 Messerschmitt Me 163B-1 Komet rocket-powered interceptor fighters are used operationally for the first time, attacking a formation of U.S.A.A.F. B-17 Flying Fortresses.

August 28 The U.S.A.A.F.'s 78th Fighter Group claims the destruction of a Messerschmitt Me 262, the first jet-powered aircraft to be shot down in air combat.

September First operational use of the Arado Ar 234B Blitz in a reconnaissance role.

September 1 The Germans begin to launch their V1 flying bombs against targets in Europe.

September 4 German V1 attacks on Britain from cross-Channel launching sites come to an end.

September 5-6 Start of the German Operation *Zeppelin*, an unsuccessful attempt to assassinate Stalin. The task group is flown

from near Riga, Latvia, to a point near Moscow by an Ar 232B transport of KG 200.

September 8 Two German V2 ballistic rockets land in Paris. Later that day, the first of these weapons launched against England detonates in Chiswick, West London, killing two people and injuring several others.

Basic specifications for a Volksjäger (People's Fighter) are drawn up by the German Air Ministry and issued to seven leading aircraft manufacturers

October First unpowered test flight of the Yokosuka MXY-7 Ohka manned rocket-powered suicide weapon, Allied SW Pacific reporting name 'Baka'.

October 23 Beginning of the Battle of Leyte Gulf, during which the Japanese introduce the use of Kamikaze attacks by suicide planes, these sinking the U.S.S. *St. Lo* and several other vessels. When the battle had ended (October 25) the Japanese had lost three battleships, 10 cruisers and 11 destroyers, marking the end of the Japanese fleet as an effective fighting force.

October 27 Mission flown by the U.S.A.A.F.'s 9th Fighter Squadron from Tacloban airstrip marks the first U.S. air operation from the Philippines since 1942.

November 1 A U.S.A.A.F. F-13 (a reconnaissance variant of the B-29 Superfortress) is the first U.S. aircraft to fly over Tokyo since the Doolittle raid of 1942. (q.v. April 18, 1942)

1944 Marking the 50th anniversary of the fighter's participation in the Allied D-Day assault, this U.S.A.A.F. Lockheed P-38J Lightning fighter took six years to restore from 1986

1944 Kamikaze by Dwight Shepler (courtesy U.S. Department of the Navy)

1945 Mistel 2 composite of II/KG 200

November 3 Start of the Japanese 'Fu-Go Weapon' (balloon bomb) offensive against the U.S.A. (q.v. May 22, 1945)

November 12 The 52,600-ton German battleship *Tirpitz*, anchored in Tromsø Fjord, Norway, is sunk by bombs dropped from Avro Lancasters of the R.A.F.'s Nos. 9 and 617 Squadrons.

November 15 A first flight is made by the Boeing XC-97 Stratofreighter prototype (43-27470).

November 24 First major bombing attack on Tokyo from the Mariana Islands by 88 B-29s of the U.S.A.A.F.'s 21st Bomber Command.

December The TR-1 (VDR-3), the first Soviet turbojet engine, reportedly completes its official bench running tests.

December 6 A first flight is made by the Heinkel He 162V-1 Salamander turbojet-powered fighter prototype (200 001) at Vienna-Schwechat.

December 7 The U.S.S. *Chourre* is commissioned as the U.S. Navy's first aviation repair ship.

December 17 The U.S.A.A.F.'s 509th Composite Group, assembled to carry out U.S. atomic bomb operations, is established in Utah.

Maj. Richard Ira Bong, the U.S.A.A.F.'s most successful fighter pilot of the Second World War, scores his 40th and final victory.

December 18 First vertical launch of the German unmanned Bachem Ba 349 Natter, intended for operational use as a manned, vertically-launched rocket-powered interceptor.

1945

January 1 In Operation *Bodenplatte* the Luftwaffe, in its last major attack, attempts to destroy the maximum number of Allied aircraft on the ground. About 800 Luftwaffe aircraft are involved in this surprise air strike. A total of 465 Allied aircraft are destroyed or damaged and more than 220 Luftwaffe aircraft are lost during this operation.

February 13–15 R.A.F. and U.S.A.A.F. night and day attacks on Dresden, Germany, create a devastating fire storm which virtually destroys the city. The estimates as to the number of dead vary between 35,000 and 220,000.

February 17 The softening-up of Iwo Jima, which is the most strongly defended of all Japanese positions, begins with a combined attack from carrier-based aircraft naval heavy guns and U.S. Seventh Air Force B-24 Liberators.

February 19 With massive air and sea support, the U.S. Marines begin landing on Iwo Jima.

February 21 First flight is made by the Hawker Sea Fury prototype (SR661), which proves to be the last piston-engined fighter to serve in FAA first-line squadrons.

The U.S. Navy aircraft carrier *Saratoga* is hit and badly damaged by Kamikaze attack.

February 22 Some 9,000 Allied aircraft make a concentrated attack on the German transport system.

February 23 The Luftwaffe sinks its last ship of the war, the *Henry Bacon* belonging to convoy RA.64.

February 25 First flight is made by the Bell XP-83 prototype, a pressurized turbojet-powered escort fighter developed from the P-59 Airacomet.

February 28 First manned flight test of the vertical take-off Bachem Ba 349 Natter (Viper) rocket-powered target defence interceptor kills the pilot, Oberleutnant Lothar Siebert. Three subsequent manned launches in March are successful, and the Natter is approved for operational use.

March 9 Allied aircraft provide support in operations against German armour attempting to eliminate the Remagen bridgehead, established two days previously.

In one of the first attacks by the Luftwaffe's Mistel 2 composites of II/KG 200, which operates Junkers Ju 88Gs and Focke-Wulf Fw 190s as the lower and upper components respectively, four composites strike the Görlitz bridges spanning the Neisse.

March 9/10 In a change of tactics, more than 300 Marianas-based B-29 Superfortresses armed with incendiary bombs make a low-altitude night attack on Tokyo.

March 11 Allied air forces make an all-out bombing attack on Essen to cut German rail communications prior to the Rhine crossings.

March 14 First operational use of the 22,000-lb (9,979kg) 'Grand Slam' bomb, dropped by a Lancaster of No. 617 Squadron on the Bielefeld Viaduct, Germany.

March 16 The U.S. Navy claims that in attacks on Japanese bases during the previous month they have destroyed 648 enemy aircraft.

Organized Japanese resistance on Iwo Jima ends. U.S. Marine casualties total 6,891 dead and 18,070 injured, but this small island is to prove a valuable emergency landing field for bomber aircraft attacking the Japanese homeland. By the war's end, 2,251 B-29 Superfortresses have found refuge there.

March 17 Following the success of the first incendiary attack on Tokyo, 307 B-29s drop 2,300 tons of incendiary weapons on Kobe, Japan.

March 18 First flight of the Douglas XBT2D-1 Skyraider prototype, a single-seat carrier-based dive-bomber/torpedo-bomber, which is the first aircraft of this category to be used by the U.S. Navy. It enters service too late to see operational use during the Second World War.

More than 1,250 bombers plus an escort of some 670 fighters make the U.S.A.A.F.'s biggest daylight attack on Berlin.

March 20/21 Luftwaffe aircraft attack Britain. This was the last German attack on the U.K. by piloted aircraft.

March 21 The first but unsuccessful sortie is made by the Japanese Yokosuka Ohka purpose-built suicide aircraft.

1945 Messerschmitt Me 262A-1a

March 21–24 The Allied air forces in Europe mount a large-scale attack against the Luftwaffe and its bases. This great strategic effort virtually destroys the Luftwaffe as an effective force.

March 27 The last V2 rocket falls on Britain, at Orpington, Kent.

March 31 The British Commonwealth Air Training Plan is officially terminated. It has produced 137,739 trainees, including 54,098 pilots.

April 1 Scoring their first major success, Japanese Ohka suicide aircraft severely damage the battleships U.S.S. *West Virginia* and three other vessels. One of them is the British aircraft carrier *Indefatigable*.

April 7 While making a final effort to try and hamper U.S. landings on Okinawa, the 71,000-ton Japanese battleship *Yamoto*, a cruiser, and four of eight destroyers are sunk by endless attack from U.S. Navy carrier-based aircraft.

The U.S.A.A.F. is able to begin fighter-escorted B-29 missions against targets on the Japanese homeland.

April 10 The last Luftwaffe wartime sortie over Britain is made by an Arado Ar 234B turbojet-powered reconnaissance aircraft operating from Norway.

In an attack on targets near Berlin, the U.S.A.A.F. loses 19 of its bomber aircraft and eight escort fighters to attacks by Messerschmitt Me 262 turbojet-powered fighters.

April 12 The American destroyer U.S.S. *Mannert L. Abele* is sunk by a Japanese Ohka suicide aircraft off Okinawa.

April 19 First flight is made of the de Havilland Sea Hornet prototype (PX212). When the type enters service post-war, it is the first twin-engined single-seat fighter to be operated from aircraft carriers of the Royal Navy.

The International Air Transport Association (IATA) is formed at Havana, Cuba, succeeding the International Air Traffic Association.

April 23 The U.S. Navy's PB4Y Liberators of Patrol Bombing Squadron 109 launch two Bat missiles against Japanese shipping in Balikpapan harbour, Borneo. This is the first known combat use of automatic homing missiles during the Second World War.

April 26 Flying a Fieseler Fi 156 Storch, Hanna Reitsch carries Gen. Rittel von Greim from Berlin–Gatow into Berlin. There he is promoted by Hitler to command the Luftwaffe, replacing Hermann Goering.

April 28 Benito Mussolini is captured at Dongo, near Lake Como, and shot by Italian Communist partisans.

April 29 War in Italy comes to an end, with German envoys signing terms of unconditional surrender.

R.A.F. Bomber Command begins airdrops of food and clothing to the Dutch people. Some 6,600 tons are supplied in just over a week.

May 7 R.A.F. Coastal Command sinks its 196th and last German submarine of the Second World War, the U-320, by No. 210 Squadron, west of Bergen.

Documents for the unconditional surrender of all German forces are signed at General Eisenhower's headquarters.

The unconditional surrender of the German forces is ratified in Berlin, and the war in Western Europe ends officially at midnight.

May 22 It is announced in the U.S. that the Japanese have been attempting to attack the continental United States by means of balloons carrying incendiary material. Released in Japan, they were carried by jet streams across the Pacific.

May 29 The advance party of the U.S.A.A.F.'s 509th Composite Group (the atom bomb team) arrives in the Mariana Islands.

May 31 BOAC and Qantas begin a joint weekly Hurn, Hampshire to Sydney, NSW service with Lancastrian aircraft.

June 11 B-29s of the U.S.A.A.F.'s 393rd Very Heavy Bomber Squadron, the only combat aircraft of the 509th Composite Group, land at Tinian, Marianas.

June 17 The U.S.A.A.F.'s 21st Bomber Command begins a series of incendiary attacks on all major Japanese towns.

June 25 National Skyway Freight Corporation is established in the U.S.A. First all-cargo airline in the U.S., in early 1946 it adopts the title of Flying Tiger Line Incorporated.

July 2 The Japanese begin a major evacuation of the people of Tokyo, due to continuous and devastating air attacks.

July 5 The United States CAB authorizes American Overseas Airlines, Pan American and TWA to operate over the North Atlantic.

July 10 The final U.S. Navy aircraft carrier actions of the Second World War begin, the ship-based aircraft attacking targets on the Japanese homeland.

July 14 Attacking Japanese-held oilfields at Boela, Ceram Island, U.S.A.A.F. Douglas A-20s from Hollandia make the first use of rocket bombs in the southwest Pacific

July 15 The R.A.F.'s 2nd Tactical Air Force is reformed as the British Air Force of Occupation, Germany.

July 16 Major Gen. Curtis LeMay takes command of the U.S.A.A.F.'s 20th Air Force.

July 20 The 393rd Squadron of the 509th Composite Group begins making practice bombing attacks against Japanese cities, using conventional HE bombs.

July 21 Japanese forces in Burma are decimated by air attack from Mustangs and Spitfires as they attempt to cross the Sittang river.

July 25 Gen. Carl Spaatz is instructed that the 509th Composite Group should make its first atom bomb attack on Japan as soon as possible after August 3, 1945.

July 30 The Mediterranean Allied Air Forces are disbanded.

August 1 851 aircraft are deployed against targets in Japan in the largest operation mounted by B-29 Superfortresses.

August 2 The operational orders for the atom bomb attack are signed. Hiroshima is named as the primary target, with Kokura or Nagasaki as alternatives.

August 6 The B-29 Superfortress *Enola Gay*, captained by Col. Paul W. Tibbets Jr., drops the world's first operational atomic bomb over the city of Hiroshima.

August 7 Japan's first turbojet-powered aircraft makes its first flight as the Nakajima J8N1 Kikka Special Attack Fighter prototype.

August 9 Lieutenant Robert H. Gray of the Royal Canadian Navy Volunteer Reserve, the pilot of a Corsair fighter-bomber, is killed attacking a Japanese destroyer. Attached to the Fleet Air Arm, he is posthumously awarded the last Victoria Cross to be won during the Second World War.

The second atomic bomb is dropped over Nagasaki from the B-29 *Bock's Car* captained by Maj. Charles W. Sweeney.

August 14 Flying its last wartime mission, the U.S.A.A.F.'s 20th Air Force despatches 754 B-29s and 169 fighters to attack targets in Japan.

August 15 Seven Japanese suicide aircraft make the last Kamikaze attack of the war.

Andrei G. Kochetkov, Head of NII-VVS Fighter Test section, becomes the first Soviet pilot to fly a jet-powered aircraft – a captured Me 262A fighter at Shcholkovo near Moscow.

August 19 Two Mitsubishi G4M Betty transports carry the Japanese surrender delegation to Ie Shima.

August 21 All existing contracts under the U.S. Lend-Lease Act are cancelled.

August 27 B-29 Superfortresses airdrop supplies to Allied prisoners of war in the Weihsien camp near Peiping, China.

September A captured Fa 223 Drache becomes the first helicopter to cross the English Channel, flown by its ex-Luftwaffe aircrew to Brockenhurst, Hampshire.

September 2 Surrounded by the U.S. Pacific Fleet, the Japanese surrender documents are signed aboard the battleship U.S.S. *Missouri* anchored in Tokyo Bay.

September 10 The U.S.S. *Midway*, the first of the U.S. Navy's 45,000-ton class carriers, is commissioned at Westport News, Virginia.

September 15 Spitfires lead a formation of some 300 R.A.F. fighters in the first Battle of Britain anniversary fly-past over London.

September 29 Swissair resumes operations to the U.K., making a first post-war flight on its Zurich–London route.

October 4–8 Qantas operates its first post-war flight to Singapore, flown by the C-class flying-boat Coriolanus (VH-ABG).

October 22 Sabena resumes operations on its Brussels–London route.

Air France's Paris–London route is reopened.

October 23 American Overseas Airlines inaugurates post-war transatlantic routes using Douglas DC-4 airliners.

November 6 Flying a mixed power plant Ryan FR-1 Fireball, which has a conventional piston-engine plus a turbojet engine in the aft fuselage, Ensign J.C. West uses the latter engine only to make the first turbojet-powered landing on an aircraft carrier, the U.S.S. *Wake Island*.

November 7 Flying a Gloster Meteor F.4, Gp. Capt. H.J. Wilson establishes a first post-war aircraft world speed record of 606.25mph (975.67km/h).

November 10 BOAC and South African Airways inaugurate a joint 'Springbok' service between Hurn, Hampshire, and Johannesburg.

November 30 The U.K. Air Transport Auxiliary is disbanded. During the course of the war, its pilots had ferried 307,378 aircraft.

December 3 The third prototype of the de Havilland Vampire 1 (LZ551), which had been modified for deck landing trials aboard the H.M.S. *Ocean*, becomes the first pure jet aircraft in the world to operate from an aircraft carrier.

December 4 A Lockheed Constellation of TWA sets a record transatlantic flight time for a commercial aircraft making the first scheduled service from Washington to Paris.

December 8 A first flight is made by the prototype Bell Model 47 helicopter.

1946

January 1 Heathrow, which is to become the site of the future London Airport, is handed over from the Air Ministry to the Ministry of Civil Aviation.

The British European Airways Division of BOAC (BEA) is established to take over the U.K.–Europe services which had been operated by No. 110 Wing, 46 Group, R.A.F. Transport Command.

The flying restrictions that had been imposed in the U.K. at the beginning of the Second World War are rescinded.

January 10 A U.S. Army Sikorsky R-5 sets an unofficial helicopter height record of 21,000ft (6,400m) at Stratford, Connecticut.

January 19 A first unpowered flight is made by the Bell X-1 research aircraft, following launch from a Boeing B-29 Superfortress 'motherplane'.

January 26 The U.S.A.A.F. establishes its first experimental guided missile group at Eglin AFB, Florida.

January 31 BOAC resumes its flying-boat services from the U.K. to Singapore.

February 4 Pan American flies its first scheduled Constellation flight from La Guardia, New York to Hurn, Hampshire in a flight time of 14 hrs 9 mins.

February 10 A Consolidated Liberator (AM920) completes BOAC's 2,000 transatlantic crossings of the Return Ferry Service.

February 28 The Republic XP-84 Thunderjet prototype makes its first flight from Muroc Dry Lake.

March 4 BEA begins operations with its aircraft in civil markings and its crews in BOAC uniform.

March 8 The Bell Model 47 is granted the first commercial helicopter certificate to be awarded by the U.S. CAA.

March 10 After RMA Berwick arrives at Baltimore, Maryland, BOAC ends transatlantic operations with Boeing Model 314s.

March 21 The U.S.A.A.F. establishes its Air Defense Command, Strategic Air Command, and Tactical Air Command.

April 24 First flights of the Yakovlev Yak-15 (one Jumo 004B) and Mikoyan MiG-9 (two BMW 003A) jet fighter prototypes, the first pure jet Soviet aircraft to fly.

May 31 London's Heathrow Airport (formerly Heathrow Airfield) is officially opened. Its facilities include one runway and several tents for passenger handling.

June 1 A Pan American Constellation lands at London Heathrow on the airline's first scheduled New York–London service.

June 14 BOAC's last scheduled service from Hurn Airport, Hampshire.

June 22 Two U.S.A.A.F. Lockheed P40 Shooting Star fighters carry the first U.S. airmail to travel by turbojet-powered aircraft, from Shenectady to Washington D.C. and Chicago, Illinois.

June 25 First flight of the first Northrop XB-35 at Muroc, the world's first full-size flying-wing bomber intended for service (though cancelled after a further 13 development aircraft had been built). (q.v. October 21, 1947)

July 1 BOAC inaugurates a twice-weekly London–New York service operated with the Lockheed Constellation.

In an exercise codenamed Operation *Crossroads*, a U.S.A.A.F. B-29 drops an atomic bomb over 73 naval vessels anchored at Bikini Atoll in the Pacific Ocean.

July 21 The McDonnell XFH-1 Phantom becomes the first pure turbojet aircraft to operate from a U.S. aircraft carrier, the U.S.S. *Franklin D. Roosevelt*.

July 24 Bernard Lynch makes the first recorded manned ejection from an aircraft on the ground, a Gloster Meteor, by means of a Martin-Baker ejection seat. It is reported that ejections were made from German jet aircraft during the Second World War.

July 25 Just over ten years after his death, Brigadier Gen. William 'Billy' Mitchell is posthumously awarded the U.S. Congressional Medal of Honor.

July 31 SAS (Scandinavian Airlines System) is formed in a unique post-war collaboration of the national airlines of Denmark, Norway and Sweden.

August 1 British European Airways Corporation is established, primarily to operate routes in the British Isles and to Europe.

August 8 The first prototype of the giant Corsair XB-36 bomber (42-13570) makes its first flight.

August 17 Sgt. L. Lambert, U.S.A.A.F., becomes the first person in the U.S. to make a manned test of an ejection seat from a Northrop P-61 Black Widow flying at 300mph (483km/h) at 7,800ft (2,375m).

September 11–12 First post-war meeting of the Fédération Aéronautique Internationale (FAI).

September 16 Alitalia (Aerolinee Italiane Internazionale) becomes incorporated in Italy. BEA was initially a 40 per cent shareholder.

September 19 TAP (Transportes Aéreos Portugueses SARL), which had been formed as a division of the government's Civil Aeronautics Secretariat during 1944, becomes established as an airline and inaugurates its first Lisbon–Madrid service on this date.

September 24 Cathay Pacific Airways is incorporated in Hong Kong, originally as a small charter airline.

September 27 The de Havilland DH.108 sweptwing research aircraft breaks up in the air over the Thames estuary killing the pilot, Geoffrey de Havilland Jr.

September 29–October 1 A U.S. Navy Lockheed P2V Neptune crewed by Cmdr. T. Davis and E. P. Rankin sets a new non-stop world distance record of 11,235.6 miles (18,081.99km) flying from Perth, Australia to Columbus, Ohio.

October 1 Beginning of the first U.S. experiments of airmail delivery in the Chicago suburbs are made by the U.S. Post Office in conjunction with the U.S.A.A.F., using Sikorsky helicopters.

October 6 The first non-stop Hawaii–Egypt flight over the North Pole is made in a U.S.A.A.F. Boeing B-29, covering a distance of 10,873 miles (17,498km).

November 1 The U.S. Navy non-rigid airship XM-1 completes a flight of 170 hrs 3 mins which is a world record for flight unsustained by any form of refuelling.

December 9 The first powered flight is made by a Bell X-1 rocket-powered research aircraft.

1947

March 14 Saudia (Saudi Arabian Airlines Corporation), which had been formed by the Saudi Arabian government during 1946, begins scheduled operations.

April 1 JAT (Jugoslovenski Aerotransport) is established by the Yugoslavian government as the national airline.

April 4 The International Civil Aviation Organization (ICAO) is established, with headquarters in Montreal, Canada.

April 15 BOAC begins a weekly Constellation service between London and Montreal, this being BOAC's first commercial operation to Canada.

May 28 British South American Airways begins a series of non-stop flight refuelling trials over a route from London to Bermuda. These are flown by the Avro Lancaster G-AHJV, which is flight-refuelled by an Avro Lancaster tanker over the Azores.

First full flight is made by the Douglas D-558-1 Skystreak research aircraft from Muroc Dry Lake, California. The Skystreak later establishes two world speed records, the first on August 20, 1947, flown by Cmdr. T.F. Caldwell, U.S. Navy, at a speed of 640.60mph (1,030.95km/h). The second record is made five days later, by Major M. E. Carl of the U.S.M.C., at a speed of 650.78mph (1,047.33km/h).

June 17 Pan American inaugurates a nearly-round-the-world service, flown the long way round from New York to San Francisco.

1946 Northrop XB-35

June 19 A new world speed record of 623.61mph (1,003.60km/h) is set by Col. Albert Boyd flying a Lockheed P-80R Shooting Star at Muroc Dry Lake, California.

July 2 The first Mikoyan I-310 (Type 'S') jet fighter prototype makes its first flight. This forerunner of the MiG-15 is believed lost in a flying accident, but a second prototype is more successful. (q.v. December 30, 1947)

July 16 The Saunders-Roe SR.A/1, the world's first turbojet-powered flying-boat, makes its first flight. An experimental fighter, it is the first flying-boat to be flown at a speed in excess of 500mph (805km/h).

July 24 The first flight of the Ilyushin Il-22, the first Soviet jet-powered bomber. The design is unsuccessful and flight tests are terminated soon afterwards.

July 26 President Truman signs the United States Armed Forces Unification Act.

July 27 The Tupolev Tu-12, the first Soviet turbojet-powered bomber to gain production status, makes its first flight.

August 3 First public appearance during the Soviet Aviation Day parade of the Tupolev Tu-4 heavy bomber, a direct Soviet copy of the Boeing B-29 Superfortress. (q.v. July 29, 1944)

August 10 BEA inaugurates a scheduled all-cargo service. This is operated by Douglas DC-3s over a route from London to Prague via Brussels.

August 14 Following the partition of India, the Royal Pakistan Air Force is established on this date. It becomes the Pakistan Air Force on March 23, 1956.

September 18 Foundation date of the United States Air Force, which becomes an independent service within the new united U.S. armed services.

September 22 A U.S.A.F. Douglas C-54 Skymaster makes a fully-automatic flight from Stephenville, Newfoundland to the U.K.

October 1 Los Angeles Airways inaugurates its first scheduled helicopter airmail services operated by Sikorsky S-51s.

The first flight is made by the North American P-86 Sabre prototype (NA-140), which becomes the U.S.A.F.'s first sweptwing fighter (redesignated F-86 Sabre).

October 14 Piloted by Capt. Charles Yeager, the Bell X-1 *Glamorous Glennis* rocket-powered research aircraft becomes the first in the world to exceed the speed of sound in level flight, attaining Mach 1.06 or 700mph (1,126km/h) at 42,000ft (12,800m).

1947 Douglas D-558-1 Skystreak

October 21 The first Northrop YB-49 flying-wing heavy bomber, powered by eight 4,000-lb (1,814kg) Allison J35-A-5 turbojets, makes its first flight.

November 1 BEA operates its last scheduled services from Croydon Airport, Surrey.

November 2 The eight-engined Hughes H-4 Hercules, the largest flying-boat ever built, makes its one and only flight over Los Angeles harbour, covering a distance of about 1 mile (1.6 kilometres).

December 1 Qantas operates its first through service from Sydney, NSW to London's Heathrow Airport, flown by the Lockheed Constellation *Charles Kingsford Smith* (VH-EAD).

December 17 On the 44th anniversary of the Wright brothers' first flight, the prototype of the Boeing XB-47 swept-wing jet bomber (46-065) makes its first flight from Boeing Field, Seattle, to Moses Lake AFB.

December 30 First flight of the second Mikoyan Type 'S' fighter prototype powered by an imported Rolls-Royce Nene 2 turbojet. After successfully passing its State Acceptance tests the fighter is assigned the designation MiG-15, its entry into service giving the Soviet Air Force an early performance lead in turbojet-powered fighters.

1948

January 30 The death is announced of Orville Wright, at Dayton, Ohio at the age of 76.

February 4 The U.S.A.F. Military Air Transport Service (MATS) is established.

February 18 The Spanish airline Aviaco (Aviación y Comercio SA) is established to operate all-cargo services, but turns to scheduled passenger operations during 1950.

March 23 A new world altitude record of 59,445ft (18,119m) is set by John Cunningham flying a de Havilland Vampire I from Hatfield, Hertfordshire.

April 3 Alitalia operates its first post-war service to the U.K. with the inauguration of its Rome–London route.

April 5 Growing transatlantic passenger traffic is highlighted by a BOAC announcement that its Lockheed Constellations have made 1,000 North Atlantic crossings.

April 14 The official opening of the Southampton, Hampshire flying-boat terminal by the U.K. Minister of Aviation shows that, so far as the U.K. is concerned, the age of the flying-boat has not passed.

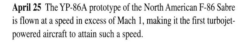

1947 Saunders-Roe SR.A/1

1947 Capt. Charles Yeager in Glamorous Glennis

April 25 The YP-86A prototype of the North American F-86 Sabre is flown at a speed in excess of Mach 1, making it the first turbojet-powered aircraft to attain such a speed.

May 20 The Israeli air force is in action against Arab forces for the first time.

May 23 The U.S.A.F. announces the activation of a new wind tunnel at Aberdeen, Maryland, with a test section having a continuous capability of 3,000mph (4,828km/h).

May 27 It is announced in the U.K. that the government had awarded a £100,000 tax-free payment to Air Cdre. Frank Whittle for his pioneering work on aircraft turbojet engines.

June 1 BEA begins the first helicopter public airmail service in the U.K., operated by Westland/Sikorsky S-51s from Peterborough, Cambridgeshire, to points in East Anglia.

June 18/19 All road traffic between Berlin and West Germany is stopped at midnight by the Soviet military authorities.

June 24 Due to so-called 'technical reasons', all rail services between Berlin and West Germany are terminated by the Soviet military authorities.

June 26 A first airlift of supplies into Berlin is organized by the U.S.A.F. using C-47s based near Frankfurt, marking the beginning of the Berlin Airlift.

June 28 The first British and international Class G helicopter record is established by Sqdn. Ldr. Basil H. Arkell, flying the Fairey Gyrodyne G-AIKF at an average speed of 124.31mph (200.06km/h).

British air operations in connection with the Berlin Airlift begin.

July 16 First flight of the Vickers Viscount prototype (G-AHRF) is made at Wisley, Surrey. On its entry into service it becomes the world's first turboprop-powered civil transport.

July 20 A first west-east crossing of the North Atlantic by turbojet-powered aircraft is recorded by 16 Lockheed F-80 (formerly P-80) Shooting Star fighters. They complete a flight from Selfridge Field, Michigan, to Scotland.

July 23 The U.S.A.F.'s Military Air Transport Service is ordered to establish an Airlift task force for, if necessary, the long-term sustenance of Berlin.

August 4 British independent civil operators become involved in the Berlin Airlift.

August 16 First flight of the Northrop XF-89 Scorpion prototype at Edwards AFB, California. When the type enters service during 1950 it becomes the U.S.A.F.'s first all-weather turbojet-powered interceptor.

August 21 Douglas C-54 Skymasters of the U.S.A.F.'s MATS begin operations on the Berlin Airlift.

August 23 A first free flight is made by the McDonnell XF-85 Goblin prototype. It is intended to be used as a parasite escort fighter, carried by the giant Convair B-36; but subsequent analysis shows the concept to be of little worth.

September 1 First flight of the Swedish Saab J-29, which becomes the first European sweptwing jet fighter to enter operational service, in May 1951. The late 'F' production version eventually introduces an afterburning engine and air-to-air missiles.

September 6 The de Havilland DH.108 research aircraft becomes the first British aircraft to exceed the speed of sound, recording more than Mach 1 in a dive.

September 14 Royal Australian Air Force crews join operations on the Berlin Airlift.

September 15 Flying an F-86A Sabre at Muroc Dry Lake, California, Maj. R.L. Johnson, U.S.A.F., establishes a new world speed record of 670.84mph (1,079.61km/h).

October 15 The R.A.F. and U.S.A.F. combine their efforts as an Airlift task force.

October 16 South African Air Force crews join operations on the Berlin Airlift.

November 3 Royal New Zealand Air Force crews join in the continuing Berlin Airlift.

November 15 El Al Israel Airlines is formed, beginning operations from Tel Aviv to Paris and Rome in mid-1949.

1948 Saab J-29Fs (courtesy Saab/J. Thuresson)

November 22 Growing concern about the sale of Rolls-Royce turbojet engines to the Soviet Union leads to questions being raised in the U.K. Parliament, a deal which had been approved by Stafford Cripps.

November 30 First commercial use of FIDO (fog dispersal system) at Blackbushe, Surrey, to allow an urgent take-off by a Vickers Viking in thick fog.

December 8 A U.S.A.F. Consolidated B-36 completes a 9,400-mile (15,128km) unrefuelled non-stop flight from Fort Worth, Texas to Hawaii and return.

December 29 The U.S. Defense Secretary announces that work has been initiated on 'an earth satellite vehicle program'.

1949

January 3 The U.S.A. introduces a bill to speed guided missile research.

February 4 The U.S. CAA authorizes the use of GCA (ground-controlled approach) radar as a primary landing aid in bad weather.

February 14 BEA begins the first U.K. helicopter night airmail experiments, flown with Westland/Sikorsky S-51s.

February 24 In the U.S.A., Project *Bumper* sees the first completely successful two-stage rocket launch into space, reaching a height of 244 miles (393km).

February 26–March 2 The first non-stop round-the-world flight is made by the U.S.A.F.'s Boeing B-50 Superfortress *Lucky Lady II*, piloted by Capt. James Gallagher. The aircraft is flight-refuelled four times during its 94-hr 1 min, 23,452-mile (37,742-km) flight.

March 30 A bill is authorized in the U.S.A. for the establishment of a permanent radar defence network.

April 2 Trans-Australia Airlines takes over responsibility from Qantas for several services, including the Flying Doctor services operated from Charleville and Cloncurry.

April 4 The North Atlantic Treaty Organization becomes established following signature of the treaty by 12 nations at Washington. It becomes effective on August 24, 1949.

April 16 Peak day of the Berlin Airlift; within 24 hours, 1,398 sorties are made, carrying a total of 12,940 tons.

April 21 An R.A.F. Sunderland lands on the Yangtse River, taking a doctor and medical supplies to the British frigate H.M.S. *Amethyst* following an attack on it by Chinese Communists.

April 26 Completion of a flight-refuelled world endurance record in the U.S., made by Bill Barris and Dick Reidel flying the Aeronca Chief lightplane *Sunkist Lady*. During flight, fuel and food is hauled up four times daily from a Jeep speeding below. The Chief was kept airborne for 1,008 hrs 1 min (one minute over six weeks).

May 12 The Soviet Union ends its blockade of Berlin, but the Allied airlift continues until September 30, 1949 (q.v.), in order to build up stocks in the city.

May 13 The English Electric Canberra prototype (VN-799) makes its first flight at Warton, Lancashire. It becomes the first jet bomber to be produced in the U.K. and the first to serve with the R.A.F.

May 14 Aérolineas Argentinas is established to operate domestic and international routes.

May 18 The first New York helicopter station is established at Pier 41, East River.

May 19 The U.S. Navy flying-boat *Marshall Mars*, flying from Alameda, Idaho to San Diego, California, carries a new record total of 301 passengers plus a crew of seven.

May 21 A Sikorsky S-52 helicopter establishes a new helicopter altitude record of 21,220ft (6,468m) over Stratford, Connecticut.

June 3 Pan American introduces Boeing Model 377 Stratocruisers on its North Atlantic services. Others later go to Northwest Airlines, United Air Lines, American Overseas Airlines, BOAC and SAS.

June 26 After one year of the Berlin Airlift, about 1.8 million tons of supplies have been airlifted into the city. Outsize items have included a steam roller and 3.5-ton (3.56-tonne) girders.

July 27 The de Havilland DH.106 Comet 1 prototype (G-ALVG) makes its first flight at Hatfield, Hertfordshire.

August 1 The SBAC (Society of British Aircraft Constructors) Challenge Cup race, open to jet-powered aircraft from any nation, is won by Sqdn. Ldr. T.S. Wade flying the Hawker private-venture P.1040 prototype (VP401). Won at an average speed of 510mph (821km/h), one lap was flown at 562.5mph (905.3km/h).

August 9 In the U.S.A., the first use of an ejection seat for emergency escape from an aircraft is recorded. It is made by Lt. J.L. Fruin, U.S. Navy, from a McDonnell F2H-1 Banshee flying in excess of 575mph (925km/h) near Walterboro, South Carolina.

1949 De Havilland Comet 1 G-ALVG

1949 Boeing Model 377-10-30 Stratocruisers

September 4 The Avro 707 (VX784) makes its first flight from Boscombe Down, Wiltshire. This first British delta-wing research aircraft had been built to test the wing configuration of the future Vulcan bomber.

The Bristol Brabazon I prototype (G-AGPW), the largest landplane ever constructed in Great Britain, makes its first flight.

September 23 The Soviet Union detonates its first atomic bomb and thus ends the U.S. nuclear monopoly.

September 30 Allied aircraft end the Berlin Airlift. During the 15 months that it had been operated, almost 2.25 million tons of supplies and equipment had been flown into Berlin.

October 17 BEA begins the first night helicopter airmail service in the U.K. Flown by Westland/Sikorsky S-51s between Peterborough, Cambridgeshire and Norwich, Norfolk, the service continues until mid-April 1950. (q.v. February 14, 1949)

November 7 First flight of the Sikorsky S-55 helicopter prototype at Stratford, Connecticut. It is the first helicopter to have the centre fuselage free from a power plant installation, it being mounted instead in the fuselage.

November 18 A C-74 Globemaster I of the U.S.A.F.'s MATS lands at Marham, Norfolk, after a non-stop flight from the U.S. It carries a total of 103 passengers and crew which is then the largest number of people carried across the North Atlantic in a single flight.

1950

January 23 The U.S.A.F. Research and Development Command is established.

February 1 The U.S.A.F.'s Continental Air Command is directed to establish a civil Air Raid Warning system.

April 12 L. Welch makes the first cross-Channel sailplane flight from London to Brussels.

April 24 A DH.106 Comet 1 establishes a new London–Cairo point-to-point record en route to Khartoum and Nairobi for tropical trials.

May 9–19 In connection with the British Industries Fair, Westland Helicopters (in conjunction with Rotor Stations Ltd.) operates the U.K.'s first scheduled helicopter passenger services. These are flown between London and Birmingham using a Westland/Sikorsky S-51.

May 17 The U.S. airline Transcontinental & Western Air (TWA), which had been established during 1930, changes its name to Trans World Airlines (TWA) to reflect the world-wide operations of the company.

June 1 BEA inaugurates the world's first scheduled and sustained helicopter service. This is flown between Liverpool and Cardiff, operated by Westland/Sikorsky S-51s and continues until March 31, 1951.

June 25 The Korean War begins, with North Korean forces making a dawn crossing of the 38th Parallel borderline into South Korea.

June 27–28 The United Nations Security Council calls upon its member nations to assist South Korea in any way possible.

July 3 The first U.S. jet fighter to be involved in air combat is a Grumman F9F-2 Panther of the U.S. Navy. This is flown off the aircraft carrier U.S.S. *Valley Forge* to enter action against North Korean forces.

July 24 The first rocket is launched at the Cape Canaveral test range, this being a V2 first stage with a WAC Corporal as its second, known as Bumper-WAC. (q.v. February 24, 1949)

July 28 The world's first certificate of airworthiness for a turbine-powered civil airliner is awarded to the Vickers V630 Viscount.

July 29 The Vickers V630 Viscount G-AHRF is used by BEA to inaugurate the world's first scheduled service to be flown by a turboprop-powered airliner. The type is introduced for a short period on the airline's London to Paris service.

August 15 Using the V630 Viscount which has been operating the London–Paris route, BEA provides a London–Edinburgh service for just over a week. This is the first U.K. domestic service to be flown by a gas-turbine-powered airliner.

September 22 Colonel David C. Schilling, U.S.A.F., lands at Limestone, Maine, after a non-stop flight from the U.K. in a Republic EF-84E Thunderjet fighter. Two of these aircraft had been converted by Flight Refuelling Ltd. for refuelling by its probe and drogue system which is being adopted by Tactical Air Command. It is by using this system for three inflight refuellings that the Thunderjet records the first non-stop crossing of the North Atlantic by a turbojet-powered fighter aircraft.

September 29 At Holloman AFB, New Mexico, Capt. Richard V. Wheeler makes a parachute jump from a height of 42,449ft (12,938m).

November 7 Replacing Solent flying-boats with Handley Page Hermes aircraft on its U.K.–Johannesburg service, BOAC brings to an end the flying-boat services that had been operated by the airline and its predecessors for some 26 years.

November 8 The first victory to be scored in the first allied combat is by Lt. Russell J. Brown Jr., U.S.A.F. 51st Fighter-Interceptor Wing, flying a Lockheed F-80C. His victim is a Mikoyan MiG-15 jet fighter of the Chinese People's Republic Air Force.

November 9 In the first encounter between U.S. Navy jet fighters and MiG-15s, Lt. Cmdr. W.T. Amen flying a Grumman F9F-2 Panther becomes the first U.S. pilot to destroy another jet fighter in combat.

December 17 North American F-86A Sabres go into action in Korea with the 4th Fighter-Interceptor Wing. In their first day of combat operations, four MiG-15s are claimed as destroyed.

1951

January 1 Reinforced by some 400,000 Chinese troops, the North Koreans begin a new major advance into South Korea.

February 5 The U.S.A. and Canada jointly announce the intention to set up a DEW (distant early-warning) system for North America.

February 21 In flying from Aldergrove, Northern Ireland to Gander, Newfoundland, an English Electric Canberra B. Mk 2 becomes the first jet aircraft to fly the North Atlantic non-stop and unrefuelled. The distance of 2,072 miles (3,335km) is flown in 4 hrs 37 mins.

April 18 An Aerobee research rocket carrying a monkey in a special capsule for a space biology experiment is launched from Holloman AFB, New Mexico.

May 18 First flight of the Vickers Valiant prototype (WB210). The type is to become the first of the R.A.F.'s V-bombers to enter service.

May 20 Capt. James Jabara, an F-86 Sabre pilot of the U.S.A.F.'s 4th Fighter-Interceptor Wing in Korea, becomes the first jet pilot to score five confirmed victories over jet aircraft, destroying his 5th and 6th MiG-15s on this date.

May 29 The first solo transpolar flight is made by American C. Blair, flying a North American P-51 Mustang from Bardufoss, Norway to Fairbanks, Alaska.

July 20 The first flight of the first of three Hawker Hunter prototypes (WB188) is made from Boscombe Down, Wiltshire.

August 15 Two of BEA's DC-3s are given Rolls-Royce Dart turboprop power plant for engine development flying. They are used by BEA on cargo services between Northolt, Middlesex and Hanover, Germany, and the service which starts on this date is the first cargo service to be flown by turboprop-powered aircraft.

August 22 The Supermarine Attacker enters service with the FAA's No. 800 Squadron at Ford, Sussex. It is the first jet fighter to be standardized in the FAA's first-line squadrons.

September 20 The U.S.A.F. makes a first successful recovery of animals which have been launched into space by a research rocket. The payload of a monkey and 11 mice is recovered with no apparent ill-effects.

October 3 Squadron HS-1, the U.S. Navy's first ASW helicopter squadron, is commissioned at Key West, Florida.

November 26 First flight of the first of three Gloster Javelin prototypes (WD804). When the type enters service with the R.A.F. in early 1956, it is the R.A.F.'s and the world's first twin-jet delta-winged fighter. It is also the first R.A.F. fighter designed specifically for all-weather operations.

December 17 The U.S.A.F. claims that during the previous 12 months its No. 4 Fighter-Interceptor Wing in Korea, operating with F-86 Sabres, had destroyed 130 MiG-15s.

1952

January 3 First flight of the Bristol Type 173 prototype (G-ALBN) at Filton, near Bristol. This is the first twin-rotor, twin-engined helicopter to be designed and flown in Britain.

January 5 Pan American inaugurates its first transatlantic all-cargo service, this being operated by Douglas DC-6s.

January 22 The de Havilland Comet 1 gains the first certificate of airworthiness to be awarded to a turbojet-powered airliner.

April 15 First flight of the Boeing YB-52 prototype (49-231), which does not enter service with the U.S.A.F. until late 1957. A strategic heavy bomber, it is designed to carry nuclear weapons to any target in the world.

May 2 The de Havilland DH.106 Comet 1 (G-ALYP) flies BOAC's inaugural jet service between London and Johannesburg. This is the world's first regular-scheduled airline service to be operated by a turbojet-powered aircraft.

June 17 The U.S. Navy takes delivery at Lakehurst, New Jersey, of the world's largest non-rigid airship. Designated ZPN-1, it has an overall length of 324ft (98.76m) and a maximum diameter of 35ft (10.67m).

July 3 BOAC begins Comet 1 proving flights on its London–Tokyo route.

July 13–31 Two Sikorsky S-55 helicopters, flown in stages, achieve the first west-east crossing of the North Atlantic by helicopters.

July 19 The U.S.A.F. announces that for periods of over three days it has successfully flown free balloons at controlled constant altitudes in the stratosphere.

July 29 The first non-stop transpacific flight by a jet aircraft is completed by a North American RB-45, a reconnaissance version of the B-45 Tornado light tactical bomber. This is flown from Elmendorf AFB, Alaska, to Yokota AB, Japan.

August 11 BOAC inaugurates a weekly London–Colombo service with Comet 1s.

August 20 The first giant Saunders-Roe S.R. 45 Princess flying-boat (G-ALUN) is launched at Cowes, Isle of Wight. It flies two days later. It is intended to accommodate 105–220 persons. The giant aircraft has a 219ft 6-in (66.9-m) wing span and is powered by ten 3,780 shp Bristol Proteus 2 turboprop engines.

August 30 The Avro Vulcan B.1 prototype (VX770) makes its first flight. This large delta-wing long-range bomber is the second of the R.A.F.'s V-bombers.

September 30 A Bell GAM1-63 Rascal air-to-surface missile is launched for the first time.

October 3 The first British atomic bomb is detonated over the Monte Bello Islands, off north-western Australia.

October 14 BOAC introduces Comet 1s on its London–Singapore route, reducing the scheduled time by more than 50 per cent.

October 26 A first shadow on the de Havilland Comet's horizon occurs when BOAC's G-ALYZ is severely damaged in a take-off accident at Rome. A similar accident to a Canadian Pacific Comet during March 1953 gives proof that if the nose is held a little too high on take-off the aircraft cannot attain flying speed. Remedial action includes the installation of drooped-wing leading-edges.

October 28 First flight of the Douglas XA3D-1 Skywarrior carrier-based attack-bomber prototype. When the A3Ds begin to enter service in March 1956, they are the heaviest aeroplanes used as standard equipment aboard aircraft carriers.

November 2 A U.S. Navy Douglas F3D Skyknight destroys a MiG-15, the first time a jet fighter successfully intercepts another jet at night.

November 3 The first flight is made by the Saab-32 Lansen two-seat all-weather attack fighter, powered by a Rolls-Royce Avon turbojet. Production aircraft have a Svenska-Flygmotor licence-built version of the Avon with reheat.

November 12 First flight of the Russian Tupolev Tu-95 *Bear* long-range strategic bomber, powered by huge turboprop engines with contra-rotating propellers.

November 19 SAS (Scandinavian Airlines System) makes the first unscheduled commercial airline flights over the polar regions between Europe and North America. These are flown by Douglas DC-6Bs, but it is not until 1954 that the airline operates scheduled commercial flights over this route.

December 16 The U.S.A.F. Tactical Air Force Command activates its first helicopter squadron.

December 24 The Handley Page Victor prototype (WB771) makes its first flights. This is the third and last of the long-range medium bombers for the R.A.F.'s V-bomber programme.

1952 Saunders-Roe S.R. 45 Princess (G-ALUN)

1953 Convair Sea Dart

1953

January 3 BEA takes delivery of the first of its Vickers V.701 Viscount turboprop airliners (G-ALWE).

January 6 Luftag is formed as a German airline following the closure of Luft-Hansa after the end of the war. In the following year (1954) it becomes Deutsche Lufthansa.

January 12 The U.S. Navy begins operational flight tests with its first angled-deck carrier, the U.S.S. *Antietam*.

April 9 The first flight is made by the Convair F2Y-1 Sea Dart experimental twin-jet delta-wing seaplane fighter. This uses retractable hydro-skis to take off from and land on water.

April 18 BEA begins the world's first sustained passenger service to be operated by turboprop-powered airliners. This is the airline's London–Nicosia route, the first scheduled flight being made by Viscount V.701 *Sir Ernest Shackleton* (G-AMNY).

May 2 On the first anniversary of the inauguration of Comet operations, a BOAC Comet 1 (G-ALYV) suffers structural failure and crashes near Calcutta with the loss of 43 lives.

May 4 A new world altitude record is established by W.F. Gibb, flying an English Electric Canberra to a height of 63,668ft (19,406m).

May 18 The first flight of the Douglas DC-7 piston-engined transport is made. In its DC-7C long-range version, the type is remembered as a piston-engined airliner at the peak of its development.

May 19 The American airwoman Jacqueline Cochran pilots a Canadian-built version of the North American F-86 Sabre at a speed of Mach 1.01, becoming the first woman in the world to fly faster than the speed of sound.

May 25 The first North American YF-100A Super Sabre prototype makes its first flight. It has a significant place in world aviation history as the first combat aircraft capable of sustained supersonic performance in level flight.

June 18 The world's first air disaster involving the death of more than 100 persons occurs. This is suffered by a U.S.A.F. C-124 Globemaster II which crashes after engine failure on take-off from Tachikawa AFB, Tokyo, killing 129 people.

July 7 The first international helicopter flight into central London is made by a Sikorsky S-55 operated by Sabena. This is flown from the Allée Verte Heliport at Brussels, landing at the South Bank Heliport, Waterloo.

July 13 BEA introduces a helicopter all-cargo service between London Airport and Birmingham, flown by Bristol Type 171s.

July 16 Lt. Col. W.F. Barnes, U.S.A.F., flying a North American F-86D Sabre, sets the world's first 'more-than 700mph' speed record, the FAI-ratified record being at 715.60mph (1151.64km/h).

July 17 Lt. Guy Bordelon, flying a piston-engined Vought F4U Corsair, becomes the first U.S. Navy pilot involved in the Korean War to score five confirmed victories.

July 27 After a little over three years of fighting, the Korean War terminates with the signature of Armistice terms.

August 25 Following successful tests carried out during May 1953, the U.S.A.F. announces that the Convair B-36 bomber, in a GRB-36F configuration, is able to launch and retrieve Republic GRF-84F Thunderflash reconnaissance aircraft from an under-fuselage trapeze. About 12 of these bombers are converted to the GRB-36F configuration, enabling them also to launch and control missiles in support of development programmes.

August 27 The first flight of the first production de Havilland Comet 2 (G-AMXA) is made at Hatfield, Hertfordshire.

September 1 The Belgian airline Sabena inaugurates the first scheduled international helicopter services, flown from Brussels to link with Maastricht and Rotterdam in the Netherlands, and Lille in France.

September 7 Flying a Hawker Hunter 3, Sqdn. Ldr. Neville Duke, R.A.F., establishes a new world speed record off Littlehampton, West Sussex of 727.48mph (1,170.76km/h).

September 11 The U.S.A.F. announces that the Sidewinder air-to-air missile has made its first completely successful interception, destroying the Grumman F6F Hellcat drone that was its target.

October 1 Japan Air Lines becomes reorganized and adopts this, its current title.

October 3 Lt. Cmdr. J. B. Verdin, U.S.N., flying a Douglas F4D-1 Skyray at Salton Sea, California, sets a new world speed record of 752.78mph (1,211.48km/h).

October 24 The first flight is made by the Convair YF-102A Delta Dagger prototype from Edwards AFB, California. When it enters service in April 1956, initially with the 327th Fighter Interceptor Squadron, it is the U.S.A.F.'s first delta-wing aircraft.

November 29 The Douglas DC-7 enters scheduled airline service in the U.S.A. with American Airlines.

December 12 Capt. Charles Yeager flies the air-launched Bell X-1A rocket-powered high-speed research aircraft at a speed of Mach 2.435, or approximately 1,650mph (2,655km/h), at an altitude of 70,000ft (21,340m).

December 29 ICAO announces that for the first time the world's airlines have carried more than 50 million passengers during the preceding 12 months.

1954

January 10 The BOAC Comet 1 G-ALYP, en route from the Far East to London, breaks up in the air. The wreckage falls into the Mediterranean about 10 miles (16 km) south of Elba, but none of the 35 persons on board survives. Immediately the news of the Comet accident is received, BOAC grounds its Comet fleet for the completion of airworthiness checks.

February 28 The first flight is recorded by the first prototype Lockheed XF-104 Starfighter air superiority fighter. When it enters service in early 1958 its Mach 2 performance and wing span of just under 22ft (6.71m) causes the Press to refer to it as the 'missile with a man in it'.

March 17 BOAC announces that 20 new Comet 4s have been ordered from de Havilland; these will allow the carriage of full payload over the North Atlantic route.

March 20 The de Havilland Sea Venom enters service with No. 890 Squadron which re-formed at Yeovilton, Somerset on this date.

March 23 After inspection reveals no apparent fault in BOAC's Comet fleet, they are returned to service.

April 1 An R.A.F. photo-reconnaissance Spitfire makes the last operational sortie of the type while on duty in Malaya.

April 8 BOAC's Comet 1 G-ALYY breaks up and falls into the sea south of Naples with the loss of its passengers and crew. The type is immediately withdrawn from service and subsequent investigation reveals metal fatigue problems adjacent to windows in the pressurized structure, causing an explosive decompression.

May 1 The U.S.A.F. forms an Early Warning and Control Division, using specially-equipped RC-121C and RC-121D (later EC-121C/D) aircraft for radar surveillance.

May 25 A U.S. Navy ZPG-2 airship flown by Cmdr. M.H. Eppes and crew lands at Key West, Florida, after being airborne for just over 200 hours.

July 1 Following Japanese-U.S. agreement on the formation of defence forces for Japan, the three air arms become officially established with U.S. aid. They comprise and are still known as the Japan Air Self-Defence Force (Koku Jiei-tai), Japan Maritime Self-Defence Force (Kaijoh Jiei-tai) and the Japan Ground Self-Defence Force (Rikujye Jiei-tai).

July 15 The Boeing Model 367-80 turbojet-powered prototype of a flight refuelling tanker transport for the U.S.A.F. makes its first flight. It is to be built extensively for the U.S.A.F. as the C-135/KC-135, and to be developed as the Boeing Model 707 civil transport.

August 2 The first free flight is made by the Rolls-Royce test rig that is built to evaluate the potential of jet lift for vertical take-off and the means of controlling such a vehicle in flight. It is dubbed the 'Flying Bedstead' by the Press.

August 3 The second prototype of the Convair XF2Y-1 Sea Dart exceeds a speed of Mach 1 in a shallow dive, thus becoming the first water-based aircraft in the world to exceed the speed of sound.

August 4 The first flight is made by the first English Electric P.I.A. prototype (WG760), later to become known as the Lightning. When production aircraft enter service in December 1959, the Lightning is the R.A.F.'s first true supersonic fighter able to exceed the speed of sound in level flight.

1954 Rolls-Royce 'Flying Bedstead'

August 26 A height of about 90,000ft (27,430m), then the greatest height attained by a piloted aircraft, is set by the Bell X-1A research aircraft over the Mojave Desert.

September 1 The U.S.A.F. Continental Air Defense Command is established, with its headquarters at Colorado Springs.

September 29 The first flight of a McDonnell F-101A Voodoo is made at Edwards AFB, California. This supersonic single-seat fighter has been developed for the U.S.A.F. from the company's XF-88 Voodoo.

October 17 The Sikorsky XH-39 helicopter sets a new world altitude record for rotary-wing aircraft of 24,500ft (7,468m).

October 23 The Western nations agree to terminate occupation of West Germany and to fully incorporate the German Federal Republic into NATO.

November 1 The U.S.A.F. retires all its Boeing B-29 Superfortresses that are serving in a bomber capacity.

November 2 The Convair XFY-1's first transitions from vertical to horizontal flight and vice versa are accomplished. (q.v. August 3, 1954)

November 11 Fairey Aviation announces that its Delta 2 research aircraft has exceeded a speed of Mach 1 in a climb.

November 25 Malev (Magyar Légiközlekedesi Vállalat) becomes established as the Hungarian state airline. This follows acquisition by the Hungarian government of the Soviet Union's holding in the original Maszovlet airline, which had been formed with Soviet assistance in March 1946.

1955
The Regulus I nuclear or conventionally armed surface-to-surface attack missile is first tested. It becomes operational on some U.S. Navy aircraft carriers, cruisers and submarines from 1955, being finally phased out (from submarines) in 1965.

February 26 Ejecting from a North American F-100 Super Sabre after the controls had jammed, the company's test pilot George F. Smith becomes the first man in the world to live after ejection from an aircraft travelling at supersonic speed, in this case Mach 1.05.

March 25 The first flight is made by the first of two Ling-Temco-Vought (LTV) XF8U-1 Crusader prototypes. The last fighter designed by the Chance Vought company before becoming a component of the LTV organization, this carrier-based fighter has an unusual variable-incidence wing.

April 1 Lufthansa, the re-established German airline, flies its test domestic service from Hamburg.

April 15 A Convair CV-340 makes the first post-war landing in the U.K. by a German-operated civil airliner. This is Lufthansa's D-ACAD on a Hamburg–London proving flight.

April 17 London (Heathrow) Airport Central becomes operational, the first departure made by a BEA Viscount.

May 16 Germany's newly-formed Lufthansa begins European international (as opposed to domestic) airline operations.

May 27 The first of two Sud-Est Aviation SE.210 Caravelle prototypes makes its first flight. The Caravelle is the first multi-engined monoplane airliner to preserve a clean wing uncluttered by engine installations, its two Rolls-Royce Avon turbojets mounted in pods, one on each side of the rear fuselage.

June 3–4 Canadian Pacific Air Lines inaugurates a polar route, linking Sydney, Australia with Amsterdam, Netherlands via Vancouver. The first service is flown by Douglas DC-6B *Empress of Amsterdam* (CF-CUR).

June 15 The first Tupolev Tu-104 prototype (SSSR-L5400), a turbojet-powered civil transport, makes its maiden flight. The first jet airliner to be flown by Aeroflot, its entry into service from September 1956 completely revolutionizes many of the airline's routes.

June 29 The Boeing B-52 Stratofortress enters service with the U.S.A.F., initially with the 93rd Bomber Wing at Castle AFB, California.

July 13 The U.S.A.F. gives authorization to the Boeing Airplane Company to proceed with the development and production, in the government-owned plant at Renton, Washington, of a civil transport version of the KC-135 tanker/transport. This new airliner is to become known as the Boeing Model 707.

July 26 Egypt's President Nasser announces that the international company controlling the Suez Canal is to be terminated and the operation of the Canal nationalized. This follows U.S. withdrawal from a plan to help finance construction of the Aswan Dam, Nasser intending that revenue from the Canal should finance building of the dam.

August 1 The U.S. begins its first zero-gravity research experiments, using Lockheed T-33 trainers to study the effects of weightlessness.

August 20 Flying a North American F-100C Super Sabre from Edwards AFB, California, Col. H.A. Hanes sets a new world speed record of 822.09mph (l,323.03km/h).

August 29 A new world altitude record of 65,889ft (20,083m) is established in the U.K. by W.F. Gibb flying an English Electric Canberra.

1955 TWA Lockheed L-1049G Super Constellation

September 3 The first parachute escape from an aircraft travelling at speed on the ground is made by Sqdn. Ldr. J.S. Fifield, R.A.F. This is made to test a Martin-Baker ejection seat installed in a modified Gloster Meteor which is travelling at about 120mph (194km/h) at the moment of ejection.

October 16 During the course of experimental flights, Boeing's Model 367-80 flies non-stop from Seattle, Washington, to Washington D.C. in 3 hrs 58 mins and back to Seattle in 4 hrs 8 mins. These times represent average speeds of 589mph (947km/h) and 564mph (907km/h) respectively.

October 19 The U.S. Federal Communications Commission authorizes the American Telephone and Telegraph Company to work on a computer-controlled defence radar and communications system known as Semi-Automatic Ground Environment (SAGE).

October 22 The Republic YF-105A Thunderchief prototype makes its first flight. This supersonic single-seat fighter-bomber is to prove of great value to the U.S.A.F. during subsequent operations in Vietnam.

October 25 The first flight is recorded in Sweden by the Saab-35 Draken prototype, a double-delta-winged supersonic single-seat fighter.

November 1 A United Air Lines DC-6MB explodes in mid-air and crashes near Longmont, Colorado, killing all 44 occupants. It is subsequently established as one of the most bizarre accidents in aviation history, caused by a bomb introduced onto the aircraft by John G. Graham, intended to destroy the aircraft and his mother who is a passenger. Her death is planned to allow him to claim heavy compensation from large-scale pre-flight insurance.

Frst guided missile cruiser, the U.S.S. *Boston*, is commissioned by the U.S. Navy.

Having been responsible for placing a requirement with Lockheed in 1939 for a transcontinental airliner that instigated the design of the original Constellation that had to wait until December 1945 to make a civil transatlantic proving flight, TWA (formerly Transcontinental & Western Air) subsequently puts the improved L-1049G Super Constellation into service on the Atlantic route on this date. Not the first Super G on the Atlantic route, it was nevertheless probably the most famous service. (q.v. December 4, 1945)

December 19 An agreement is concluded between Aeroflot and BEA covering the mutual operation of air services between the Soviet Union and the U.K.

1956

January 10 The first U.S.-built rocket engine with a thrust in excess of 400,000lb (181,437kg) is run successfully for the first time at Santa Susana, California.

January 11 The U.K. Air Ministry announces the formation of a task force to conduct British atomic tests off the Monte Bello Islands in the Indian Ocean.

January 17 The U.S. Department of Defense for the first time publicly reveals the existence of the SAGE defence system. (q.v. October 19, 1955)

February 17 The first flight is made by the first production Lockheed F-104A Starfighter, a single-seat air superiority fighter for service with the U.S.A.F.

February 24 The Gloster Javelin all-weather fighter enters service with the R.A.F.'s No. 46 Squadron at Odiham, Hampshire.

March 10 Pushing the world speed record upwards by almost 310mph (500km/h) in a single jump, Lt. Peter Twiss establishes the world's first over 1,000mph speed record. This is accomplished flying the Fairey Delta 2 research aircraft off the English coast at Chichester, West Sussex, and gaining a record ratified at 1,131.76mph (1,821.39km/h).

March 14 The first successful launch is made from Cape Canaveral of a Chrysler Redstone or Jupiter-A tactical bombardment missile. This has been developed in the U.S.A. by a team headed by Dr. Werner von Braun, the designer of Germany's V2 (A4) rocket of the Second World War.

May 21 A U.S. hydrogen bomb, the first to be released from an aircraft, is detonated over Bikini Atoll in the Pacific.

June 20 The U.S. Navy commissions its first helicopter assault carrier, the U.S.S. *Thetis Bay.*

July 7 The de Havilland Comet 2 enters service with R.A.F. Transport Command at Lyneham, Wiltshire, becoming the world's first turbojet-powered aircraft to see service in a military transport role.

July 24 The first flight is made by the French Dassault Étendard IV prototype which has been built by the company as a private venture. Failing to enter production as a land-based strike fighter for which it had been intended, it is developed into a successful carrier-based fighter-bomber/reconnaissance aircraft.

July 26 Egypt seizes control of the Suez Canal from the privately owned Suez Canal Corporation.

August 23–24 A specially-prepared Hiller H-21 ('Flying Banana') twin-rotor helicopter of the U.S. Army becomes the first rotary-wing aircraft to complete a non-stop transcontinental flight from San Diego, California to Washington, D.C.

August 31 The first production example of the Boeing KC-135A tanker/transport for the U.S.A.F. makes its first flight.

September 2 A Vickers Valiant records the first non-stop transatlantic flight to be made by one of the R.A.F.'s V-bombers, from Lowring, Maine, to Marham, Norfolk.

September 7 The Bell X-2 research aircraft is flown by Capt. Iven C. Kincheloe to an altitude of 126,200ft (38,466m).

September 15 The Tupolev Tu-104 turbojet-powered airliner enters service with Aeroflot, initially on its Moscow–Irkutsk route.

September 20 The American Jupiter C rocket is first launched, attaining a record height of 682miles (1,097km).

September 24 Formation date of the post-war German air force, the Luftwaffe der Deutschen Bundesrepublik.

September 27 The Bell X-2 is destroyed in a fatal accident following a flight in which its pilot, Capt. Milburn Apt, U.S.A.F., had achieved a speed of Mach 3.2, the highest then recorded by a manned aircraft.

October 10 NACA discloses that a speed of Mach 10.4 has been attained by a four-stage research rocket.

October 11 The first atomic bomb to be dropped by a British aircraft is released by a Vickers Valiant of No. 49 (Bomber) Squadron over Malalinga, South Australia.

October 24 In secret meetings, an Anglo-French-Israeli agreement is reached to co-ordinate military operations against Egypt. This requires Israel to pose a threat to the security of the Suez Canal, thus precipitating Anglo-French intervention.

October 29 Israeli forces begin their planned attack to threaten the Suez Canal, making an airdrop of paratroops at Mitla Pass in the Sinai Peninsula.

October 30 An Anglo-French ultimatum calls upon Egyptian and Israeli troops to cease fighting and allow British and French troops to occupy key points to secure the safety of the Suez Canal.

October 31 Following rejection of the ultimatum by Egypt and Israel, British and French air forces begin attacks on Egyptian air bases.

November 5 British and French paratroops are airdropped at Port Fuad and Port Said, Egypt.

November 6 An Anglo-French amphibious landing at Port Said, carried out with air cover, is followed by a midnight cease-fire.

November 8 Ascending from Rapid City, South Dakota, Lt. Cmdr. M.L. Lewis, U.S. Navy, and Malcom D. Ross establish a world altitude record for manned balloons of 76,000ft (23,165m).

November 11 The first flight is made at Fort Worth, Texas, of the Convair XB-58 Hustler prototype, a four-turbojet delta-wing medium bomber. When the B-58 enters service in early 1960 it is the U.S.A.F.'s first supersonic bomber.

November 12 A Sikorsky S-56 helicopter in service with the U.S. Marine Corps records a speed of 162.7mph (261.8km/h).

November 17 The first flight is made by the Dassault Mirage III prototype, a delta-wing high-altitude interceptor/fighter.

December 13 In the U.S.A.F.'s altitude research chamber at its Air Research and Development Command, Dayton, Ohio, Maj. Arnold I. Beck attains the equivalent of a flight altitude of 198,770ft (60,585m).

December 26 Convair's F-106A Delta Dart prototype makes its first flight. This supersonic delta-wing all-weather interceptor is to become an important weapon of the U.S.A.F.

1957

January 18 Three of the U.S.A.F.'s Boeing B-52 Stratofortresses, commanded by Major Gen. Archie J. Old Jr., make the world's first round-the-world non-stop flight by turbojet-powered aircraft. This is completed in 45 hrs 19 mins at an average speed of 534mph (859km/h).

March 15 A U.S. Navy ZPG-2 airship, with Cmdr. J.R. Hunt and crew, establishes a new unrefuelled endurance record of 264 hrs 12 mins.

April 2 The Short SC.1 VTOL research aircraft with five Rolls-Royce RB.108 turbojets, four being used for jet-lift, makes its first flight in a conventional take-off mode.

April 4 The first flight is made by the first of three English Electric P.1B prototypes (XA847), upon which is based the production version of the Lightning.

May 15 A Vickers Valiant of the R.A.F.'s No. 49 (Bomber) Squadron drops the U.K.'s first thermonuclear (hydrogen) bomb over the Pacific, close to Christmas Island.

May 30 The U.S.A.F. discloses development of the Hughes Falcon air-to-air guided missile armed with a nuclear warhead.

July 31 The North American DEW line early warning system, extending across the arctic areas of Canada, is reported to be fully operational.

August 1 A joint U.S.-Canada North American Air Defense Command (NORAD) is informally activated.

August 19–20 Ascending from Crosby, Minnesota, Maj. David G. Simons, U.S.A.F., sets a balloon world altitude record of 101,516ft (30,942m).

August 21 The Soviet R7 rocket is successfully launched. (q.v. October 4, 1957)

September 11 Pan American inaugurates a London–San Francisco service with Douglas DC-7Cs. This is flown via Frobisher Bay, Baffin Island, and is to become known as the polar route.

September 20 The U.S.A.F. Chief of Staff announces the development of a radar system with the capability to detect ICBMs at a range of 3,000 miles (4,830km).

September 30 Trans World Airlines inaugurates a Los Angeles–London service with Lockheed L-1649A Starliners, flying over the so-called polar route.

October 4 The Soviet Union puts into Earth orbit the world's first artificial satellite. Named *Sputnik 1* ('Fellow Traveller'), it is launched by a newly-developed R7 ICBM from the U.S.S.R.'s Tyuratam Baikonur cosmodrome.

October 16 The U.S.A.F. achieves its first successful experiment to boost a man-made object to a velocity at which it can escape from the Earth's gravitational pull. This is accomplished by a special Aerobee rocket which, at a height of 54 miles (87km), detonates a shaped charge to boost small metallic pellets to a speed of some 33,000mph (53,100km/h).

October 22 Under Operation *Far Side,* a four-stage research rocket is launched from a U.S. balloon flying at some 100,000ft (30,480m) above Eniwetok Atoll. This succeeds in travelling some 2,700 miles (4,345km) into space.

November 3 The Soviet Union launches *Sputnik 2,* carrying the dog Laika which is destined to die when its oxygen is exhausted.

November 7 Showing American TV audiences a Jupiter nose-cone which has been recovered after launch from Cape Canaveral, President Eisenhower states that the U.S. has solved the missile re-entry problem.

December 6 The first flight is made by the Lockheed L-188 Electra short-to-medium-range turboprop airliner prototype (N1881). This is achieved more than a month ahead of schedule.

The U.S.A. attempts to launch a satellite into space, but the Vanguard booster rocket explodes.

December 12 Maj. Adrian Drew, U.S.A.F., using a McDonnell F-101A Voodoo, sets a new world speed record of 1,207.34mph (1,943.03km/h).

December 17 The U.S. Atlas booster rocket is successfully launched .

December 19 BOAC introduces Bristol Britannia Srs 312s on its London–New York route, marking the first transatlantic passenger services to be operated by a turboprop airliner.

December 20 The first production example of the Boeing Model 707-120, the basic domestic version, makes its first flight.

1958

January 14–20 Qantas inaugurates the airline's first scheduled round-the-world route. The first services are flown by the Super Constellations *Southern Aurora* (VH-EAO) eastbound, and *Southern Zephyr* (VH-EAP) westbound.

January 31 *Explorer l*, the first U.S. satellite to enter Earth orbit, is launched by a Jupiter C rocket from Cape Canaveral. Travelling in an elliptical orbit, data that it transmits lead to discovery of the Van Allen radiation belts that girdle the Earth.

February 18 The U.S.A.F. discloses that an airflow speed of approximately 32,400mph (52,140km/h) has been briefly attained in the test section of a wind tunnel at Arnold Research and Development Center, Tullahoma, Tennessee.

March 17 *Vanguard 1*, the second U.S. satellite to enter Earth orbit, is launched from Cape Canaveral.

April 9 The two-man crew of a Canberra bomber which explodes over Monyash, Derbyshire, make the highest reported emergency escape from an aircraft, 56,000ft (17,070m).

April 18 In the United States, Lt. Cmdr. G.C. Watkins, U.S. Navy, establishes a new world altitude record of 76,932ft (23,449m) while flying a Grumman F11F-1Tiger. This is the last of Grumman's famous 'cat' family to serve with the U.S. Navy.

April 27 The first production de Havilland DH.106 Comet 4, for service with BOAC (G-APDA), makes its first flight at Hatfield, Hertfordshire.

May 2 Lt. Commander G.C. Watkins' two-week-old world altitude record is broken by R. Carpentier in France. Flying the Sud-Ouest SO.9050 Trident (F-ZWUM), he attains an altitude of 79,452ft (24,217m).

May 7 Maj. H.C. Johnson, flying a Lockheed F-104A Starfighter in the U.S.A., plays his part in keeping the FAI busy by setting a third new world altitude record in less than three weeks, attaining a height of 91,243ft (27,811m).

May 12 The North American Air Defense Command (NORAD), which was informally activated on August 1, 1957, is formally established with headquarters at Colorado Springs.

May 15 The Soviet Union launches *Sputnik 3*, carrying an automatic scientific lab.

May 16 The first 'over-2,000km/h' world speed record is set over southern California by Capt. W.W. Irvin, U.S.A.F. Flying a Lockheed F-104A Starfighter, he attains a speed of 1,403mph (2,259.18km/h).

May 27 The first flight is made by the McDonnell F4H-1 Phantom II carrier-based fighter and tactical strike fighter.

May 30 The first Douglas DC-8 Srs 10, a domestic version of the company's turbojet sweptwing civil transport, makes its first flight.

June 9 London's new Gatwick Airport is officially opened by H.M. Queen Elizabeth II.

August 6 The Short SC.1 VTOL research aircraft makes a first tethered vertical flight.

August 7 A de Havilland DH.106 Comet 4 on a proving flight from New York to Hatfield, Hertfordshire, completes its flight in 6 hrs 27 mins.

September 9 The Lockheed X-7, a pilotless test vehicle for ramjet engines and missile components, achieves a speed of Mach 4 following launch from a Boeing B-50. Recovery is effected after each flight by an automatically-opening parachute.

September 14 The de Havilland Comet 4 G-APDA makes a proving flight from Hong Kong to Hatfield, Hertfordshire within the day, in a night time of 16 hrs 16 mins.

September 30 U.K. commercial flying-boat operations come to an end when Aquila Airways withdraws its Southampton–Madeira service.

The U.S. National Advisory Committee for Aeronautics (NACA) issues its final report and then ceases to exist.

October 1 The U.S. National Aeronautics and Space Administration (NASA) is established to absorb the functions of NACA, and to control all U.S. non-military space projects.

President Eisenhower appoints an administrator for the newly-formed Federal Aviation Agency (FAA), which absorbs the former Civil Aeronautics Administration (CAA).

October 4 BOAC inaugurates simultaneous London–New York and New York–London services with the de Havilland Comet 4. These are the first transatlantic passenger services flown by turbojet-powered airliners.

October 11 The U.S.A.F. makes a second attempt to put a research probe in orbit around the Moon. This is *Pioneer 1B* which, because its third stage cuts out fractionally too soon, travels about 70,700 miles (113,780km) before falling back towards Earth.

October 26 Pan American inaugurates its first transatlantic services operated by the Boeing 707-121 turbojet-powered airliner.

December 18 The United States places in Earth orbit a small communications relay satellite. Carrying a pre-recorded tape, on the following day it transmits President Eisenhower's Christmas message to the nation. This is the first U.S. active communication from space.

1959

January 2 The Soviet Union launches a scientific probe named *Luna 1*, which is intended to impact on the Moon's surface. It misses its target by some 3,700 miles (5,955km), passing the Moon to enter a solar orbit.

February 11 A U.S. weather balloon climbs to a record height of 146,000ft (44,500m).

February 17 The U.S. Navy launches the weather reporting *Vanguard II* satellite into Earth orbit.

February 28 Vandenberg Air Force Base in California is used for the first time to launch a satellite, *Discoverer 1*.

March 3 The U.S. *Pioneer 4* space probe is launched in an attempt to obtain crude pictures of the Moon's surface while making a fly-past at a distance of about 20,000 miles (32,200 km). It passes the Moon at almost double this range and travels on into solar orbit.

March 13 Aviation Cadet E. R. Cook becomes the U.S. Navy's first student pilot to fly solo in a turbojet-powered trainer without prior experience in a propeller-driven aircraft.

April 6 It is announced in the U.S. that seven pilots have been selected from the nation's armed services for training as space vehicle pilots.

April 23 The U.S. Hound Dog thermonuclear stand-off missile makes a successful first flight following launch from a Boeing B-52D bomber.

May 15 The last operational flight is made by an R.A.F. Sunderland, also marking the last use of water-based aircraft by the Royal Air Force.

May 28 Two monkeys, named Able and Baker, are recovered unharmed after a 300-mile (483km) flight in a compartment in the nose-cone of a Jupiter rocket.

June 3 The American satellite *Discoverer 3* is launched carrying four mice for a biological experiment.

June 8 The first unpowered free flight of the North American X-15A high-performance research aircraft is made following launch from beneath the wing of its Boeing B-52 'mother plane'.

June 17 The first flight is made by the Dassault Mirage IV-A strategic bomber prototype.

July 13–23 A London–Paris air race, held throughout this period to mark the 50th anniversary of Louis Blériot's first crossing of the English Channel (q.v. July 25, 1909), is won by Sqdn. Ldr. Charles Maughan, R.A.F. Using a combination of two motor-cycles, a Bristol Sycamore helicopter and a Hawker Hunter T.Mk 7, his city-centre to city-centre time is a remarkable 40 mins 44 secs.

July 14 Maj. V. Ilyushin of the Soviet Union sets a new world altitude record of 94,659ft (28,852m) flying the Sukhoi T-431.

July 27 Air France introduces the Sud-Aviation Caravelle on its services to the U.K., the initial operation flown by Caravelle *Lorraine* (F-BHRB).

July 29 Qantas operates its first jet service from Sydney to San Francisco with the Boeing 707-138 *City of Canberra* (VH-EBC). This is also the airline's first scheduled transpacific flight by a turbojet-powered airliner.

July 30 The first flight is made by the Northrop N-156C prototype, which exceeds a speed of Mach 1 during this initial flight test. It is to become known internationally as the F-5 Freedom Fighter.

August 7 NASA's *Explorer 6* is launched into Earth orbit from Cape Canaveral, and is to send the first TV pictures from space.

August 17 A NASA research rocket ignites a sodium flare at an altitude of some 150 miles (240km) in a project to provide information on high-altitude wind direction and velocity and the rate of matter diffusion in the upper atmosphere.

August 24 The data capsule of an Atlas-C rocket is successfully recovered after a 5,000-mile (8,050-km) flight down-range. It provides the first cine films of Earth taken from an altitude of 700 miles (1,125km).

September 4 An unmanned U.S. scientific balloon records an altitude of some 150,000ft (45,720m).

September 9 *BigJoe*, which was NASA's test version of the Mercury astronaut capsule, is successfully recovered in the Caribbean Sea after a 1,500-mile (2,415-km) flight following launch by an Atlas rocket.

September 12 The Soviet Union's *Luna 2* space probe is launched. On the 14th it becomes the first man-made object to impact on the Moon, between the craters Archimedes, Aristillus and Autolycus.

1959 Boeing B-52 carrying Hound Dogs

1959 English Electric Lightning F.Mk 1

September 17 The second example of the North American X-15A research aircraft makes a successful first powered flight following launch from its B-52 mother plane.

September 18 The Douglas DC-8 Srs 10 turbojet-powered airliner makes its first entry into U.S. domestic service, flown by Delta Air Lines and United Air Lines.

October 4 The Soviet *Luna 3* space probe is launched towards the Moon. It is to record the first circumlunar flight, and is the first to photograph the Moon's hidden surface. The photographic images are transmitted over a TV link to Earth.

October 10 The Pan American Boeing 707-321 *Clipper Windward* inaugurates the first round-the-world passenger service by turbojet-powered airliners.

October 30 The first of an initial batch of 50 production English Electric Lightning F.Mk 1 interceptors for the R.A.F. flies. First joining the R.A.F. with No. 74 Squadron in July 1960, the Lightning gives the R.A.F. its first warplane with Mach 2 performance.

October 31 Flying a Mikoyan Type Ye-66 at Sidorovo, Tyumenskaya, Col. G. Mosolov establishes a new world speed record of 1,665.89mph (2,681.00km/h).

November 16 Capt. Joseph W. Kittinger Jr. makes a balloon ascent from White Sands, New Mexico. Having gained an altitude of 76,400ft (23,285m) in an open gondola, he parachutes to the ground, recording a free-fall of 64,000ft (19,505m).

December 4 NASA tests the Mercury capsule escape system, launching a capsule with a rhesus monkey aboard which is recovered alive and quite unharmed.

December 6 A U.S. Navy McDonnell F-4 Phantom II piloted by Cmdr. L. Flint establishes a new world altitude record of 98,556ft (30,040m).

December 9 At Bloomfield, Connecticut, a Kaman H-43B rescue helicopter, crewed by U.S.A.F. officers Maj. William J. Davis and Capt. Walter J. Hodgson, sets a helicopter altitude record of 29,846ft (9,097m).

December 14 The eight-day-old world altitude record of Cmdr. L. Flint, U.S.N., is broken by a Lockheed F-104C Starfighter piloted by Capt. J.B. Jordan to a height of 103,389ft (31,513m).

December 15 A new world speed record of 1,525.93mph (2,455.74km/h) is set by Maj. J.W. Rogers, U.S.A.F., flying a Convair F-106A Delta Dart at Edwards AFB, California.

1960

January 21 In a further low-altitude test of the Mercury escape system, NASA launches a monkey named Miss Sam. She is recovered unharmed after the escape system is activated almost immediately following launch.

February 9 The U.S.A.F. activates a National Space Surveillance Control Center at Bedford, Massachusetts.

February 13 France explodes an atomic weapon in the Sahara Desert, thus becoming the world's fourth nuclear power.

April 6 The second Short SC.1 research aircraft makes the first full transitions from vertical to horizontal flight and vice-versa by a British VTOL aircraft.

April 29 First test firing by NASA of all eight Rocketdyne H-l engines of the Chrysler Saturn 1 first stage produces a combined 1,300,000lb (589,670kg) stagic thrust.

May 6 At a first public demonstration for the Press, a U.S.A.F. Minuteman is successfully launched from an underground launch pad (not a silo) at Edwards AFB, California.

May 7 A Lockheed U-2 high-altitude reconnaissance aircraft, overflying the Soviet Union and piloted by Gary Powers, is shot down from an altitude of some 65,000ft (19,810m) by a Soviet SAM near Sverdlovsk.

May 24 The U.S. launches *Midas II* into orbit, the first early-warning satellite.

June 22 The U.S.A. becomes the first to launch a rocket carrying multiple independently-instrumented satellites.

July 20 The Short SC.1 becomes the first jet-lift aircraft to fly the English Channel.

August 12 Following successful test launches in which balloons are inflated to a large diameter in space, NASA places into orbit the *Echo 1* passive communications satellite. This is of plastic material with an aluminium film, and serves as a test vehicle for the relay of several types of communication signals.

Maj. Robert White, U.S.A.F., pilots the North American X-15A research aircraft to a height of 136,500ft (41.600m).

August 16 Following the success of his earlier parachute jump (q.v. November 16, 1959), Capt. Joseph W. Kittinger Jr., U.S.A.F., jumps from a balloon at 102,200ft (31,150m), making a free fall of 84,700ft (25,815m).

August 19 The Soviet Union's *Sputnik 5* satellite is launched into Earth orbit carrying two dogs named Belka and Strelka. They are successfully recovered after completing 18 orbits.

October 1 A U.S. BMEWS (Ballistic Missile Early Warning System) radar site becomes operational at Thule, Greenland.

October 16 Marking the end of what had once seemed to be a great success story for the British aviation industry, BOAC operates its last scheduled Comet 4 New York–London service.

October 21 The first tethered flight is made by the Hawker Siddeley P.1127 Kestrel experimental V/STOL tactical fighter.

October 24 In the worst space-related accident ever, 91 people lose their lives at the Baikonur Space Centre in the U.S.S.R. (since Kazakhstan), when an R-16 booster blows up.

November 12 Launching *Discoverer 17* from Vandenburg AFB, a restartable rocket engine is used for the first time.

1961

January 31 Extending from the last unmanned Mercury experiment on December 19, 1960, NASA launches a Mercury capsule containing a chimpanzee named Ham. Although subjected to 17g during the launch phase, Ham is successfully recovered after a 420-mile (676km) down-range sub-orbital flight, with no apparent ill effects.

March 13 The Hawker Siddeley P.1127 Kestrel experimental V/STOL tactical fighter makes its first conventional flight.

March 28 Air Afrique (Société Aérienne Africaine Multinationale) is formed as a joint venture involving Air France and several now-independent African states.

March 30 NASA pilot Joe Walker attains a height of 169,600ft (51,695m) in the North American X-15A research aircraft.

April 12 The Soviet Union staggers the world by announcing that it has launched the spacecraft *Vostok 1* into Earth orbit carrying Yuri Gagarin, the first man in space. He lands successfully after one orbit of the Earth in a total flight time of 1 hr 48 mins.

April 21 Maj. Robert White, U.S.A.F., pilots the North American X-15A during the first test flight at full throttle. A speed of 3,074mph (4,947km/h) is attained at 79,000ft (24,080m), before coasting upward to an altitude of 105,100ft (32,034m).

April 28 Col. G. Mosolov, flying a Mikoyan Ye-66A, regains the world height record for the Soviet Union at an altitude of 113,898ft (34,714m).

May 5 Alan B. Shepard becomes the first American in space, with a flight time of 15 mins 28 secs. Carried in the Mercury ballistic capsule *Freedom 7*, following launch by a Redstone rocket, this is a sub-orbital trajectory during which a height of 116.5 miles (187km) and range of 297 miles (478 km) is attained.

June 28 Announcement is made of the termination of U.S. Navy airship operations, prompted by the collapse of one of four Goodyear ZPG-3W Airborne Early Warning airships. First flown in 1958, the ZPG-3W was the largest non-rigid airship to date.

June 29 The U.S. Navy's *Transit IV* satellite is launched, the first known to carry a nuclear power source in the form of a radioisotope-powered battery.

July 1 NORAD begins the operation of SPADATS, designed to electronically catalogue all man-made space objects.

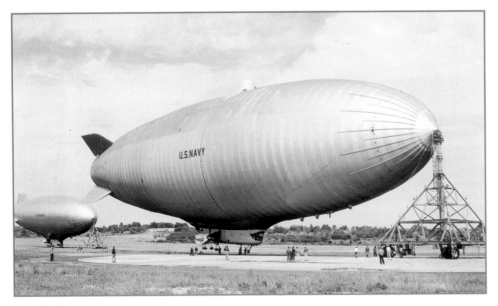

1961 Goodyear ZPG-3W

1963 Jacqueline Cochran

July 10 A Tactical Air Command pilot flies a Republic F-105D Thunderchief for more than 1,500 miles (2,410km) without any external vision. This is a test to ensure that the instrumentation and radar system of the F-105 is adequate for a squadron pilot to make a long-range IFR mission at altitudes, between 500 and 1,000ft (152 and 305m).

July 21 The U.S. puts its second man in sub-orbital flight down the Atlantic Missile Range; Virgil Grissom in the Mercury capsule *Liberty Bell 7*.

August 6 The Soviet Union launches its second man into Earth orbit in *Vostok 2*. Cosmonaut Herman Titov completes 17 Earth orbits before landing after 1 day 1 hr 19 mins.

September 13 The world-wide tracking network which has been set up for the U.S. Mercury programme is used for the first time to observe the orbit of an unmanned Mercury capsule. Data from this network convinces NASA that the Atlas is capable of putting a manned Mercury capsule into Earth orbit.

October 4 Launch of the world's first active communications satellite *Courier 1B* (U.S.A.).

November 9 In the last high-speed flight made by the X-15A during 1961, Maj. Robert White, U.S.A.F., attains a speed of 4,093mph (6,587km/h) at 101,600ft (30,970m).

November 22 At Edwards AFB, California, Lt. Col. R.B. Robinson establishes a new world speed record in a McDonnell F4H-1F Phantom II at a speed of 1,606.51mph (2,585.43km/h).

November 29 In its last unmanned Mercury capsule test, NASA launches the chimpanzee Enos into Earth orbit.

December 11 The first direct military support for South Vietnam is provided by the arrival at Saigon of a U.S. Navy aircraft carrier transporting two U.S. Army helicopter companies.

December 15 NORAD's SAGE system becomes fully operational with the completion of a 21st and final control centre at Sioux City, Iowa.

1962
January 10–11 Maj. Clyde P. Evely and crew establish a new world distance record in a Boeing B-52H Stratofortress, flying from Okinawa, Ryukyu Islands to Madrid, Spain, a distance of 12,532.3 miles (20,168.78km).

February 20 Launched by an Atlas booster, the Mercury capsule *Friendship 7* carries America's Lt. Col. John H. Glenn (U.S.M.C.) into Earth orbit (the first U.S. astronaut to go into orbit). He completes three orbits to record a flight time of 4 hrs 55 mins 23 secs before splash-down.

February 28 In the first manned test of the steel cocoon-type escape capsule carried by the General Dynamics/Convair B-58A Hustler, W.O. Edward J. Murray is ejected from the aircraft which is travelling at 565mph (909km/h) at 20,000ft (6,100m). After a 26-second free-fall, a parachute is automatically deployed, bringing him safely to the ground eight minutes after ejection.

April 30 Flown by NASA pilot Joe Walker, the North American X-15A attains a new record height of 246,700ft (75,195m).

May 24 NASA's Mercury capsule *Aurora 7* is launched into Earth orbit carrying Lt. Cmdr. M. Scott Carpenter, U.S. Navy, on a similar three-orbit mission to that of *Friendship 7*. Experiencing re-entry problems, he guides the spacecraft manually through re-entry but splashes down some 260 miles (420km) from the target area after a 4-hr 56 minute mission. He remains in his life raft until rescued.

June 27 The North American X-15A flown by NASA pilot Joe Walker attains its highest recorded speed of 4,159mph (6,693km/h).

Flying the Mikoyan Type Ye-166 at Sidorovo Tyumenskaya, Col. G. Mosolov establishes a new world speed record of 1,665.89mph (2,681km/h).

July 10 The *Telstar 1* communications satellite is placed in Earth orbit by a Delta booster from Cape Canaveral. It makes possible the first transatlantic exchanges of TV programmes, proving to 'the man in the street' that he might gain some benefit from the space race.

August 8 In tests carried out to determine the effects of kinetic heating, the second North American X-15A attains a surface temperature of 900°F (482°C) at an altitude of 90,000ft (27,430m) and speed of 2,900mph (4,665km/h).

August 11 and 12 Respective launch dates of the Soviet Union's *Vostok 3* (Andrian Nikolayev) and *4* (Pavel Popovich) into Earth orbit. The two spacecraft make a rendezvous in orbit, approaching to within 3 miles (5km) of each other. TV cameras in the spacecraft provide the first TV transmission from a manned vehicle in space.

September 29 The Canadian built and designed *Alouette 1* satellite, the first to be built outside of the U.S. or U.S.S.R., is successfully launched by a Thor-Agena B booster.

October 3 Cmdr. Walter M. Schirra, U.S.N., completes a 9 hr 13-minute space mission in the Mercury-Atlas 8 *Sigma 7*.

October 22 President Kennedy announces that U.S. reconnaissance aircraft have established that offensive missile sites are being erected in Cuba.

October 24–29 Lengthy exchanges between Kennedy and Khrushchev end the 'Cuban missile crisis'. The U.S. pledges that it will not invade Cuba and, in return, the U.S.S.R. agrees to halt construction of missile bases and remove its missiles.

December 13–14 Under the designation Project *Stargazer*, a balloon manned by Capt. Joseph W. Kittinger, U.S.A.F., carries civilian astronomer William C. White and a specially-mounted telescope to a height of 82,000ft (25,000m). This enables White to make a number of observations under ideal conditions.

December 14 NASA's *Mariner II* scans the surface of Venus for 35 mins as it flies past at a distance of 21,642 miles (34,830km). A surface temperature of 834°F (428°C) is recorded. *Mariner II* is the first man-made satellite to reach another planet.

1964 North American X-15A-2

1964 BAC TSR.2

1963

January 7 The U.S.S. *Buck*, having completed qualification trials, is the first U.S. warship to become operational with Gyrodyne GH-50C ASW drone helicopters.

January 17 NASA pilot Joe Walker flies the North American X-15A to a height of 271,000ft (82,600m). He qualifies for 'astronaut's wings', having exceeded a height of 50 miles (80km).

February 9 The Boeing 727 prototype is flown for the first time, a short/medium-range jet transport. Incorporating three rear-mounted engines and a T-tail, it is in other respects similar to the Model 707/720 that had preceded it.

April 30–12 May American airwoman Betty Miller makes the first transpacific solo flight by a woman. This is accomplished in a four-stop flight from Oakland, California to Brisbane, Australia.

May 1 Flying a Lockheed TF-104G Starfighter near Edwards AFB, California, Jacqueline Cochran successfully sets a 100-km closed-circuit world speed record for women of 1,203.686mph (1,937.14km/h).

May 15–16 In the longest U.S. space mission to date, Maj. L. Gordon Cooper, U.S.A.F., orbits the Earth 22 times in Mercury-Atlas 9 *Faith 7*. Cooper carries out experiments related to the navigation and guidance of spacecraft, is monitored by a TV camera, and makes a manually-controlled re-entry, to record a total mission time of 34 hrs 19 mins 49 secs.

June 7 Following a merger of Air Liban and Middle East Airlines, the title Middle East Airlines Air Liban is adopted.

June 14–19 The Soviet Union's *Vostok 5* spacecraft carrying Valery Bykovsky, records the longest space mission to date of 119 hours 16 minutes.

June 16 With the launch of a second spacecraft within two days, the Soviet Union's *Vostok 6* carries the first woman into space, cosmonaut Valentina Tereshkova.

July 19 NASA pilot Joe Walker flies the North American X-15A to an unofficial height record of 347,800ft (106,010m).

July 25 A nuclear test ban treaty is finalized after almost three years of discussion; subsequently signed by most nations of the world, it brings an end to tests in the atmosphere.

July 26 The U.S. *Syncom 2* is the world's first geosynchronous satellite, remaining static over the Atlantic.

August 28 The first test in the U.S. Apollo programme is made when a Little Joe II booster, which has been designed for unmanned sub-orbital testing of this vehicle, makes a first test with a dummy Apollo spacecraft.

October 1 Under the command of Rear Adm. James R. Reedy, a ski-equipped Lockheed C-130 Hercules makes a first transpolar non-stop flight from Capetown, South Africa to McMurdo Sound, Antarctica.

October 17 The United Nations General Assembly confirms earlier unilateral declarations made by the U.S. and U.S.S.R. that no weapons will be mounted in or used from space.

The *Vela Hotel* satellite makes the first detection of a nuclear explosion from space.

November 20 The U.S.A.F. formally accepts its first two McDonnell F-4C Phantom II fighters at MacDill AFB, Florida.

November 29 By an executive order, President Johnson renames Cape Canaveral Cape Kennedy, and its space facilities as the John F. Kennedy Space Center.

December 15 Alia (Alia Royal Jordanian Airline) begins operations. Formed in October 1963, it is the successor to Air Jordan.

December 17 The first flight is made by the Lockheed C-141A four-turbofan long-range military transport ordered for service with the U.S.A.F.'s MATS.

1964

January 29 Saturn I SA-5 is successfully launched, recording the first flight with a live second stage.

February 29 For the first time, President Johnson publicly reveals the existence of the Lockheed A-11 high-altitude reconnaissance aircraft.

April 8 The first unmanned Gemini spacecraft is placed in Earth orbit by a Titan II booster.

April 17 At the end of a 29-day flight in her Cessna 180 *Spirit of Columbus*, U.S. airwoman Jerrie Mock lands at Columbus, Ohio, so becoming the first woman pilot to' fly solo round the world.

May 11 Piloting a Lockheed TF-104G Starfighter, Jacqueline Cochran sets a new world speed record for women over a 15/25km course of 1,429.246mph (2,300.14km/h).

May 12 American Joan Merriam, flying a Piper Apache, becomes the second woman to make a solo round-the-world flight, taking 56 days to cover the route which had been planned by Amelia Earhart.

June 28 The North American X-15A No. 2 research aircraft which following an accident has been rebuilt with new large external fuel tanks, makes its first flight under the new designation X-15A-2.

July 27 The Daniel Guggenheim Medal for 1964 is posthumously awarded to Dr. Robert H. Goddard in recognition of his important contributions to rocket theory and design.

July 28 NASA's unmanned *Ranger 7* is launched from Cape Kennedy, subsequently taking 4,316 TV pictures of the lunar surface in the last 13 minutes of flight before it impacts on the Moon.

July 31 In the U.S.A., A.H. Parker sets the first over 646-mile (1,000km) sailplane distance record using a Sisu-lA.

1965 Canadair CL-84 Dynavert

August 5 In retaliation for the unprovoked attack by the North Vietnamese patrol boats on U.S. destroyers, President Johnson orders carrier-based aircraft from U.S.S. *Constellation* and *Ticonderoga* to attack North Vietnamese naval bases. A U.S. Navy pilot killed in the action was this service's first loss of the Vietnam War.

September 21 The North American XB-70A Valkyrie prototype makes its first flight. This Mach 3 strategic bomber programme is subsequently abandoned.

September 27 The BAC TSR.2 two-seat all-weather supersonic attack reconnaissance aircraft prototype (XR219) makes its first flight. It proves to be the only one of the type to fly as the programme is subsequently cancelled.

October 12 The Soviet Union launches the *Voskhod 1* spacecraft into Earth orbit. It is the first to carry a multiple crew consisting of Vladimir Komarov, Konstantin Feoktistov and Boris Yegorov, who are able to carry out their mission without wearing spacesuits.

October 14 The first flight is made by the Sikorsky CH-53A Sea Stallion prototype, a heavy assault helicopter accommodating up to 38 combat troops which has been developed for the U.S. Marine Corps.

October 16 The People's Republic of China detonates its first atomic bomb, becoming the world's fifth nuclear power.

October 30 NASA pilot Joe Walker makes the first flight with the Bell Lunar Landing Research Vehicle (LLRV). This has a variable-stability system that allows pilots to gain the reactions and sensations of operating in a lunar environment.

November 28 The U.S. space probe *Mariner 4* is launched. This passes within 5,400 miles (8,690km) of Mars on July 14, 1965, transmitting 21 pictures of the Martian surface.

December 14 In Operation *Barrel Roll*, U.S.A.F. fighter-bombers attack the Ho Chi Minh Trail communist supply route in Laos.

December 21 The first General Dynamics F-111A variable-geometry (swing-wing) multi-purpose fighter makes its first flight. This is carried out with the wings locked at 26° sweepback but full wing sweep, from 16° to 72.5°, is first accomplished on January 6, 1965.

December 22 President Johnson approves development by Lockheed of the CX-HLS military transport for the U.S. Air Force. This becomes the C-5A Galaxy.

December 22 The first flight is made by the Lockheed SR-71A strategic reconnaissance aircraft.

1965

January 27 The potential of geostationary satellites for emergency communications is demonstrated. For the first time, a comsat is used as a link between a Pan American Boeing 707 in flight and a remote ground control station.

February 23 The first flight is recorded by the Douglas DC-9 short/medium-range airliner, powered by two rear-mounted turbofan engines.

March 6 A Sikorsky SH-3A Sea King makes the first non-stop helicopter flight across the North American continent. Taking off from the carrier U.S.S. *Hornet* at San Diego, California, it lands on the carrier U.S.S. *Franklin D. Roosevelt* at Jacksonville, Florida having completed a distance of 2,116 miles (3,405km). This establishes a new international straight-line distance record for helicopters.

March 18 The Soviet Union launches *Voskhod 2* with cosmonauts Pavel Belyayev and Alexei Leonov. During their mission, Leonov makes the first 'spacewalk', tethered to the spacecraft while floating in space for about ten minutes.

March 23 Launched by a Titan II booster, NASA's *Gemini 3* spacecraft is placed in Earth orbit. It carries the first U.S. two-man crew, astronauts Maj. Virgil Grissom and Lt. Cmdr. John Young, on a 4 hr 53-min mission. They make the first-ever piloted orbital manoeuvre.

April 1 Tasman Empire Airways, which had become wholly nationally owned in 1961, adopts the name Air New Zealand.

April 6 The Hughes *Early Bird 1* comsat is launched into geostationary Earth orbit. When it becomes operational, on June 28, 1965, it is the world's first commercial satellite for public telephone services.

May 1 Flying a Lockheed YF-12A from Edwards AFB, California, Col. R.L. Stephens establishes a new world speed record of 2,070.11mph (3,331.507km/h).

May 7 The Canadair CL-84 Dynavert, a twin-engined tilt-wing VSTOL close-support/transport prototype, achieves its first vertical take-offs and landings.

June U.S.A.F. McDonnell Douglas F-4C Phantom II tactical fighters are first deployed to Vietnam.

June 3 The NASA spacecraft *Gemini 4* is launched into Earth orbit carrying astronauts James McDivitt and Edward White. During this mission, Maj. White makes a 21-minute spacewalk (the first by a U.S. astronaut), known in U.S aerospace terminology as an extra-vehicular activity (EVA).

1965 U.S.A.F. F-4Cs taking fuel from a KC-135 over Vietnam

August 21 NASA's *Gemini 5* spacecraft, with astronauts Gordon Cooper and Charles Conrad on board, carries out the first exploration 'long' space mission, lasting 7 days 22 hrs 56 mins. *Gemini 5* is the first manned spacecraft to use fuel cells to provide electrical power (instead of batteries).

September 7 The first flight is made by the prototype Bell Model 209 HueyCobra armed helicopter, which has been developed as a private venture for the U.S. Army from the UH-1B Iroquois.

September 13 The Fédération Aéronautique Internationale homologates its first hot-air balloon record, an altitude of 9,780ft (2,978m) attained by B. Bogan in the U.S.

September 27 The first of three evaluation LTV A-7A Corsair II single-seat carrier-based attack aircraft makes its first flight. The type is to prove a valuable addition to U.S. Navy carrier-based aircraft operating off Vietnam.

November 15 A first circumnavigation of the world, overflying both poles, is made by a Boeing 707 of the Flying Tiger Line.

November 16 The Soviet interplanetary space probe *Venera 3* is launched, later becoming the first man-made object to impact on the surface of Venus.

November 26 Using a Diamant launch vehicle, the French *Asterix 1* (Matra A1) test satellite is placed in Earth orbit. France thus becomes the first nation, other than the U.S. or U.S.S.R., to develop and orbit a satellite by its own efforts.

December 4 NASA's *Gemini 7* spacecraft is launched into Earth orbit carrying astronauts Frank Borman and James Lovell. In addition to carrying out a longer-stay mission (13 days 18 hrs 35 mins), *Gemini 7* serves as a rendezvous target for *Gemini 6*.

December 15 The *Gemini 6* spacecraft is launched with astronauts Walter Schirra and Thomas Stafford on board. Manoeuvring to within 6ft (1.8m) of *Gemini 7* in orbit, this is the first manoeuvred rendezvous in space.

1966

January 31 The Soviet Union launches the unmanned spacecraft *Luna 9*, which becomes the first man-made vehicle to soft-land on the lunar surface and transmit panoramic still pictures of the terrain.

March 16 NASA's *Gemini 8* spacecraft, carrying astronauts Neil Armstrong and Maj. David Scott, is launched into orbit to carry out docking manoeuvres with an Agena docking target. Although they achieve the first manual docking of two spacecraft in orbit, this has to be aborted almost immediately because of uncontrollable spinning.

May 18 British airwoman Sheila Scott takes off from London (Heathrow) Airport in a Piper Comanche 260B in an attempt to make a solo round-the-world flight. (q.v. June 20 1966)

May 30 NASA launches the *Surveyor 1* lunar probe, which makes the first fully-controlled soft landing on the Moon on June 2. It transmits 11,150 high-resolution pictures of the lunar surface.

June 3 NASA launches *Gemini 9* with Thomas Stafford and Eugene Cernan on board. Cernan performs a 2-hour spacewalk during the 3-day 21minute mission.

June 20 Sheila Scott lands at London (Heathrow) Airport at the conclusion of her solo round-the-world flight. She is not only the first British airwoman to complete such a flight, but she has established a new record for women of 33 days 3 minutes.

July 18–21 During the *Gemini 10* mission (Michael Collins and John Young), a scientific experiment package is retrieved from an orbiting Agena craft. This gives evidence of a capability to rendezvous with and repair/service satellites in Earth orbit.

August 2 First flight of the Soviet Sukhoi Su-17 as a variable-geometry derivative of the Su-7.

August 10 NASA launches the Lunar *Orbiter 1* unmanned spacecraft which duly goes into orbit around the Moon and obtains high resolution pictures of potential Apollo landing sites.

August 31 The first of six Hawker Siddeley Harrier development aircraft (XV276) makes its first hovering flight at Dunsfold, Surrey.

September 12 NASA launches *Gemini 11* with Charles Conrad Jr. and Richard Cordon Jr. on board, to carry out docking tests. The mission lasts 2 days 23 hrs 17 mins.

September 24 In the Soviet Union Marina Solovyeva, flying a Ye-76 (MiG-21), sets a new women's world speed record of 1,270mph (2,044km/h).

November 4 The Hawker Siddeley Trident G-ARPB, fitted with Smiths' Autoland system, makes three test landings at London Heathrow. These are made in conditions of 150-ft (46m) visibility when all other operations have been cancelled.

November 11 NASA launches *Gemini 12* with James Lovell and Edwin Aldrin on board. Three spacewalks and a docking manoeuvre are performed during the 3 day 22 hr 34 min mission.

December 23 The first flight of Dassault's Mirage F1 single-seat fighter prototype is successfully made.

1967

January 2 It is announced in the U.S. that Boeing has been awarded a contract for the design of an SST, and that General Electric is to develop the power plant for it.

January 25 Soviet *Cosmos 139* anti-satellite satellite conducts the first fractional orbit bombardment.

January 27 In a tragic accident on the ground, U.S. astronauts Roger Chaffee, Virgil Grissom and Edward White are burnt to death in a flash fire during tests of the *Apollo 1* command module. They had been scheduled to make the first Apollo orbital flight on February 21, 1967. These are the first losses of the U.S. space programme.

March 9 The Royal Aeronautical Society announces that the Kremer prize, which had been offered for a first significant man-powered flight, has been increased to £10,000 and that any nation is eligible to compete.

April 6 Trans World Airlines becomes the first of the U.S. airlines to complete the transition to an all-jet fleet.

April 9 The first flight is made by the Boeing Model 737-100 turbojet short-range transport. This basic version provides accommodation for 80–101 passengers.

April 23 Launch date of *Soyuz 1* in which Soviet cosmonaut Col. Vladimir Komarov is killed when the spacecraft crashes during the final stages of landing. He is the first man known to have died in the course of a space flight.

May 5 UK-3 (*Ariel 3*), the first all-British satellite, is launched into Earth orbit from the Western Test Range, California.

June 5 The Boeing Company delivers its 1,000th jet airliner, a Model 707-120B for American Airlines.

Outbreak of the '6-day war' between Israel and the Arab states. Pre-emptive air strikes by the Israeli Air Force make the Egyptian, Jordan and Syrian air forces virtually ineffective.

June 10 Following the enforcement of a cease-fire the '6-day war' ends. It is theoretically an Israeli victory, due largely to their skilful deployment of air power.

June 17 The Chinese People's Republic detonates its first thermonuclear weapon.

July 2 First flight of the T6-1 delta-winged prototype for the Soviet Sukhoi Su-24 Fencer variable-geometry strike bomber. (q.v. January 17, 1970)

July 7 A Pan American Boeing 707-321B (N419PA) records the first fully-automatic approach and landing by a four-engined turbojet aircraft with passengers on board.

July 21 In Operation *Pershing*, CS riot-control gas is dropped from helicopters onto suspected VC emplacements at Binh Dinh in Vietnam.

August 7 Aérolineas Argentinas and Iberia jointly inaugurate the world's longest non-stop air route, between Buenos Aires and Madrid.

1967 Chinook dropping CS riot-control gas (courtesy U.S. National Archives)

1967 Dornier Do 31E3

August 17 The U.S. lunar probe *Surveyor 3* is launched to the Moon, achieving a soft-landing in the Ocean of Storms. A mechanical scoop, activated from Earth, allows soil samples to be taken for photographic transmission to Earth and, in addition, more than 6,000 pictures are taken of the landing site.

September 8 U.S. *Surveyor 5* makes the first chemical analysis of the Moon's surface.

October 3 Flown by Maj. William Knight, U.S.A.F., the North American X-15A-2 attains its highest speed of Mach 6.72 (4,534mph or 7,297km/h).

October 20 The first emergency escape using the crew module of a U.S.A.F. F-111A is made over Texas, the two crew members remaining within the module until reaching the ground unhurt.

November 3 The U.S. Defense Secretary states that the U.S.S.R. has developed a fractional-orbit bombardment system (FOBS) that will allow orbiting satellites to release nuclear weapons against Earth targets.

November 29 Australia's *Wresat 1* research satellite, the nation's first, is launched into Polar orbit from Woomera using a modified Redstone missile as booster.

December 11 The Aérospatiale-built Concorde 001 prototype is rolled out at Toulouse, France.

December 16 The Dornier Do 31E experimental V/STOL transport makes its first transition from vertical to horizontal flight. The first transition from horizontal to vertical is made on December 21.

December 28 The first production Hawker Siddeley Harrier GR.1 (XV738) makes a 20-minute flight at Dunsfold, Surrey.

1968

January 21 A U.S.A.F. Boeing B-52 of Strategic Air Command, carrying four nuclear weapons, crashes on sea ice on its approach to Thule AFB, Greenland.

January 29 It is announced that the highly successful North American X-15 research programme is to terminate at the end of 1968.

March 17 U.S.A.F. General Dynamics F-111As are used operationally for the first time in Vietnam. Two are lost by the end of the month.

March 18 The U.K. Minister of State, Mintech, announces that talks have been held with Canadian, Dutch, German and Italian ministries to consider British participation in the design and development of a European multi-role combat aircraft (MRCA).

March 28 Col. Yuri Gagarin, Soviet cosmonaut and first man in space, is killed when the MiG-15UTI that he is flying crashes near Kirzhatsk, north of Moscow.

April 13 Martin-Baker announces that a successful ejection on that date marks the 2,000th life to be saved by the company's escape system.

April 15 The Soviet Union's unmanned spacecrafts *Cosmos 212* and *213* dock and undock automatically in Earth orbit.

April 26 The *Daily Mail*, a long-term sponsor of aviation, announces an Atlantic Air Race for 1969 to commemorate the 50th anniversary of the first non-stop transatlantic flight. Prize money is to total £45,000.

May 1 The U.K. Hot Air Group's inaugural meeting, at the Balloon and Airship Flying Centre, Blackbushe, Hampshire, is opened by an ascent of the hot-air-balloon *Bristol Belle* (G-AVTL).

May 16 Carbon-fibre-reinforced plastics turbine compressor blades are exhibited for the first time at a meeting of the Royal Society.

BOAC's Super VC 10 G-ASGK, carrying 146 passengers, makes the airline's first fully automatic approach and landing at the completion of a scheduled flight from Chicago and Montreal.

June 26 Demonstrating the development that is being made in nuclear propulsion, a Phoebus 2A nuclear reactor on test at the Nuclear Rocket Development Station, Jackass Flats, Nevada, generates a thrust of 200,000lb (90,718kg) for a 12-minute test run.

June 30 The Lockheed C-5A Galaxy makes its successful first flight at Dobbins AFB, Georgia, the largest landplane then flown.

August 24 France detonates a 2-megaton thermonuclear weapon suspended from a balloon over Mururoa Atoll.

September 8 The Anglo-French Jaguar E-01 prototype makes a successful first flight from the Centre d'Essais en Vol at Istres, France.

September 30 The Boeing Model 747 prototype, the world's first wide-body jetliner, is rolled out at Everett, Washington.

The New York City Police, which was the first police force in the world to make regular use of helicopters, celebrates the 20th anniversary of their introduction into daily use.

October 11–22 The first Apollo test mission is made, lasting for 10 days 20 hrs 9 mins. This is *Apollo 7*, launched by a Saturn 1B and carrying astronauts Walter Schirra, Don Eisele and Walter Cunningham.

October 20 Soviet satellites *Cosmos 248* and *249* undertake the first co-orbital anti-satellite trials.

October 26 The Soviet Union launches *Soyuz 3* with Georgi Beregovoi on board. The mission, which lasts 3 days 22 hrs 51 mins, includes a rendezvous with unmanned *Soyuz 2*.

November 12 NASA announces that its *Apollo 8* mission, scheduled for December 21, 1968, will put the Apollo spacecraft in orbit around the Moon.

December 21–27 The *Apollo 8* spacecraft is launched by a Saturn V booster carrying astronauts Frank Borman, James Lovell and William Anders. During its 6 day 3 hr 1 min mission, this spacecraft completes the first manned flight around the Moon (on December 24).

December 31 The prototype of the Soviet Union's Tupolev Tu-144 SST makes its successful first flight, the world's first supersonic transport aircraft to fly.

1969 First Boeing Model 747

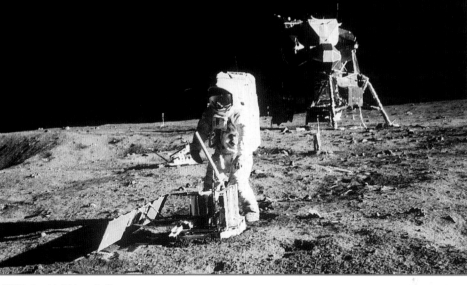

1969 Eagle, with Aldrin on the Moon

1969

January 14 and 15 Respective launch dates of the Soviet Union's *Soyuz 4* and *5* spacecraft. They accomplish the first docking of two manned spacecraft in Earth orbit and the first crew exchange carried out by EVA methods.

February 9 The Boeing Company achieves the successful first flight of the Model 747 wide-body transport. Dubbed 'jumbo-jet' by the world's Press, it is the first aircraft of this class to be flown.

February 12 Three days after the first flight of the world's largest fixed-wing civil transport, there is an announcement in the Soviet Union to the effect that Russia has developed the world's largest helicopter, the giant Mil Mi-12. This is confirmed early the following month when it is established that on February 12 the helicopter set a number of load-to-height records.

March 2 The first Sud-Aviation/BAC Concorde 001 SST prototype makes its completely successful first flight at Toulouse, France, piloted by Sud's chief test pilot André Turcat.

March 3–13 The U.S. astronauts Col. James McDivitt, Col. David Scott and Russel Schweickart are launched into Earth orbit aboard *Apollo 9*. During this mission the first in-space tests of the Lunar Module are carried out, and it is the first occasion that a crew-transfer is made between two space vehicles through an internal connection.

March 19 A weekly return service between Montreal, Canada and Resolution Bay, Cornwallis Island, is inaugurated by Nordair. This is the world's first scheduled jet service inside the Arctic circle.

March 28 BAC announces the formation by BAC, Fiat, Fokker and Messerschmitt-Bölkow of a new aerospace company. This is the international Panavia GmbH, created to develop the multi-role combat aircraft (MRCA).

April 9 The first U.K.-built SST prototype, Concorde 002, makes its successful first flight piloted by Brian Trubshaw.

April 28 A V/STOL Hawker Siddeley Harrier GR. 1 of the R.A.F. records a first transatlantic crossing by the aircraft type, flying from Northolt, Middlesex to Floyd Bennett Field, New York.

May 11 The *Daily Mail* Transatlantic Air Race ends at midnight. Beginning a week earlier to allow time for a maximum number of individual efforts, it is won by Lt. Cmdr. Brian Davis, Royal Navy, with a time of 5 hrs 11 mins 22 secs to get from the top of the Post Office Tower, London, to the top of the Empire State Building, New York.

May 18–26 The *Apollo 10* spacecraft, carrying astronauts Thomas Stafford, Eugene Cernan and John Young, carries out a Moon-landing rehearsal. While the *Apollo 10* travels in lunar orbit, Stafford and Cernan detach the Lunar Module and make two descents to within 8.7 miles (14km) of the Moon's surface.

June 15 An Ilyushin Il-62 long-range airliner is used by Aeroflot to inaugurate a joint service with Pan American, linking Moscow and New York.

July 16–24 NASA's *Apollo 11* is launched to the Moon, carrying astronauts Neil A. Armstrong, Edwin E.A. Aldrin and Michael Collins. On July 21, Neil Armstrong becomes the first man on the Moon after he and Aldrin have descended to the Moon's surface in the Lunar Module *Eagle*. The mission is completed by a successful splashdown on July 24, the total time being 8 days 3 hrs 19 mins.

July 30 NASA's *Mariner 6* interplanetary probe transmits 24 pictures of Mars, taken some 2,130 miles (3,428km) from its surface and relayed over a distance of 0.77 million miles (1.24 million kilometres).

August 16 Flying a modified Grumman F8F-2 Bearcat over a 3-km course at restricted altitude, U.S. test pilot Darryl Greenamyer sets a new world speed record for piston-engined aircraft of 477.98mph (769.23km/h). This beats by just over 8mph (13km/h) the record set by a Messerschmitt Me 209VI in 1939.

August 30 First flight of the Soviet Tupolev Tu-22M Backfire intermediate-range supersonic variable-geometry bomber, piloted by Vasili Borisov. Deliveries to the 185th Heavy Bomber Regiment of Guards at Poltava, Ukraine, begins in 1975.

October 11, 12 and 13 The respective launch dates of the Soviet Union's *Soyuz 6, 7* and *8* spacecraft, which are the first to make a group flight without docking.

October 20 Finnair becomes the world's first airline to operate aircraft with an inertial guidance system on scheduled passenger services. This dispenses with the requirement for a navigator as a member of the aircrew.

October 29 The U.S. Secretary of Defense states that as an economy measure, the U.S.A.F.'s B-58A Hustler, the world's first supersonic strategic bomber, is to be phased out of service.

November 7–10 Flying the unorthodox BD-2, James Bede sets an unrefuelled closed-circuit world distance record for piston-engined aircraft of 8,973.4 miles (14,441.26km). (q.v. December 5, 1981)

November 8 West Germany's *Azur* research satellite is launched into orbit by a NASA Scout from the Western Test Range. It is the first West German space satellite.

November 14–24 The second Moon landing is made by the *Apollo 12* mission, its all-U.S. Navy crew comprising Charles Conrad, Richard F. Gordon and Alan L. Bean. Major experiments are conducted on the Moon for the first time.

November 17 The first U.S./Soviet SALT (Strategic Arms Limitation Talks) begin in Helsinki, Finland.

December 1 The U.S. Federal Air Regulation Pt 36 is introduced, the first legislation to limit aircraft noise at airports.

December 17 The first Lockheed C-5A Galaxy for service with the U.S.A.F. is officially handed over at Marietta, Georgia.

December 18 Aircraft competing in the England–Australia Commemorative Air Race begin taking off from London's Gatwick Airport. Marking the 50th anniversary of the first England–Australia flight, and the bi-centenary of the discovery of Australia, it is won by Capt. W.J. Bright and Capt. F.L. Buxton in the Britten-Norman BN-2A Islander G-AXUD.

1969 Convair B-58A Hustlers

1970

January 12 The first Boeing Model 747 wide-body transport lands at London Heathrow, a Pan American aircraft on a proving flight from New York.

January 17 First flight of the Soviet T6-2I variable-geometry prototype to the Sukhoi Su-24 Fencer strike bomber. (q.v. July 2, 1967)

February 1 Capt. Raymond Munro makes the first hot-air balloon crossing of the Irish Sea, from Brittis Bay, Co. Wicklow to Ennerdale, Cumberland.

February 11 Japan becomes the fourth nation in the world to launch a domestic satellite using a nationally-built launch rocket, the *Ohsumi*, boosted by a Lambda 4S carrier rocket from the Kagoshima Space Centre.

March 26 The British 'Gee Chain', which provided valuable navigational services during the Second World War, is finally closed down.

April 1 Air Jamaica begins scheduled operations. This airline was formed during 1968 to succeed an earlier company of the same name.

April 11–17 NASA's *Apollo 13* mission focuses the world's attention when an oxygen tank explodes during the outward flight.

The resulting emergency is resolved by brilliant evaluation and improvisation, returning astronauts James Lovell, John Swigert and Fred Haise safely to Earth.

April 24 The Chinese People's Republic launches its first satellite into Earth orbit using an indigenous booster rocket. A basic research satellite, it is identified as *Chicom 1* by NORAD.

May 25 The U.S. Government announces that Multiple Individual Re-entry Vehicles (MIRVs), or multiple warheads, have been developed and are available for deployment on the nation's ICBMs.

June 1 The first production Lockheed C-5A Galaxy to enter operational service with the U.S.A.F. is delivered to Military Airlift Command (MAC) at Scott AFB, Charleston, Virginia.

The Soviet Union's *Soyuz 9* spacecraft is launched into Earth orbit carrying cosmonauts Andrian Nikolayev and Vitali Sevastyanov. They land successfully after completing what is then the longest space mission, totalling 17 days 16 hrs 59 mins.

July 2 The first flight is made by the Saab Sk 37 Viggen two-seat trainer prototype from the company's airfield at Linköping.

August 17 The Soviet Union launches the inter-planetary probe *Venera 7*. The instrument capsule from this probe makes the first confirmed landing on Venus in January 1971, transmitting a weak data signal for 23 minutes.

August 22 Two Sikorsky HH-53C helicopters complete a non-stop transpacific flight of some 9,000 miles (14,484km), refuelled en route by Hercules tankers.

August 29 The first flight of the McDonnell Douglas DC-10 wide-body jet (N10DC) is made at Long Beach, California.

September 12 The Soviet Union's *Luna 16* moon probe is launched. This remarkable vehicle makes an unmanned automatic soft-landing on the lunar surface and scoops up a sample of surface soil which it stores within the vehicle before taking off and returning to Earth on September 24.

Three commercial transports which had been hijacked by Arab guerrillas are destroyed by dynamite on the desert airstrip known as Dawsons's Field near Amman, Jordan. They comprise a Boeing 707 of Trans World Airlines, a McDonnell Douglas DC-8 of Swissair, and a BAC VC l0 of BOAC.

October 24 The last flight of the North American X-15 research programme is made by NASA pilot William H. Dana.

November 4 The Concorde 001 prototype attains its design cruising speed of Mach 2 for the first time. The U.K.-built 002 achieves this milestone nine days later.

November 6 The U.S.A.F. launches a military reconnaissance satellite into a geostationary orbit above the Indian Ocean. It is

reported to have sensors able to detect infra-red emissions from rocket plumes.

November 10 The Soviet Union launches the *Luna 17* moon probe. This soft-lands on the lunar surface to deploy a Lunokhod rover vehicle on November 17 which travels more than 6 miles (9.5km) during the ensuing nine months, conducting experiments and transmitting the results to Earth.

November 16 The first Lockheed L-1011 TriStar wide-body jet airliner (N1011) makes its first flight.

December 18 Aérospatiale, Deutsche-Airbus and Fokker-VFW establish Airbus Industrie to be responsible for the A300B programme.

December 21 The first flight is recorded by the prototype of the Grumman F-14 Tomcat carrier-based variable-geometry multi-role fighter for the U.S. Navy.

1971

January 22 The crew of a U.S. Navy Lockheed P-3C Orion, led by Cmdr. Donald H. Lilienthal, establish a new world long-distance record for aircraft with turboprop engines at just over 7,010 miles (11,281km). On January 27 the same aircraft sets up a speed in a straight line record at 500.89mph (806.10km/h), also in Class C, Group II.

January 31–February 9 NASA's *Apollo 14* is launched to make the third U.S. Moon landing, a mission which is successfully

1970 Recovery of Apollo 13 *on board U.S.S.* Iwo Jima *(courtesy NASA)*

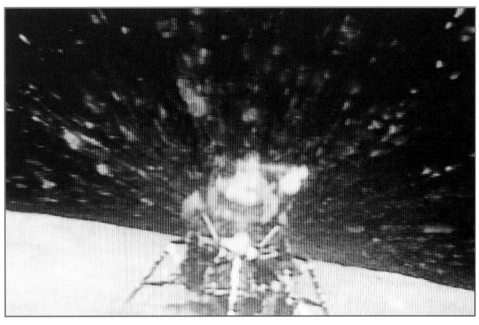

1972 Take-off from the Moon's surface of the Lunar Module Orion's *ascent stage during the* Apollo 16 *mission (courtesy NASA)*

completed by astronauts Alan Shepard, Stuart Rossa and Edgar Mitchell. It is the first landing on the Moon's highlands.

March 24 By a single vote, the U.S. Senate decides not to provide funding for development of an American SST, bringing cancellation of the Boeing 2707-300 project.

April 12 The U.S.A.F. announces the use of a so-called 'daisy cutter' bomb in Vietnam. This is a conventional high-explosive bomb designed to clear jungle areas.

April 14 Trans-Mediterranean Airways, which was formed during 1953 to provide non-scheduled freight services from Beirut, inaugurates the first round-the-world cargo service.

April 15 The U.S. Marine Corps' first Harrier squadron, VMA-513, becomes operational at Beaufort Air Station, South Carolina.

April 19 The Soviet Union launches the *Salyut 1* into Earth orbit, the first space station.

April 22–24 The Soviet Union's *Soyuz 10* spacecraft is launched into orbit, docking with *Salyut 1*, but no crew board the space station.

May 3 H.M.S. *Ark Royal* embarks the R.A.F.'s No. 1 Squadron with its Harriers for sea trials off the Scottish coast.

May 13 Concorde 001 makes its first fully automatic approach and landing at Toulouse, France.

May 20 The U.S. Supersonic Transport Program is officially terminated by Congress.

May 28 The Soviet Union launches the interplanetary space probe *Mars 3*, which subsequently puts the first data capsule on the Martian surface.

May 30 Launch date of NASA's *Mariner 9* interplanetary probe, which becomes the first artificial satellite of Mars. It transmits more than 7,000 pictures, many of which provide remarkable detail of the Martian surface.

June 6 The Soviet Union puts the *Soyuz 11* spacecraft in orbit with cosmonauts Georgi Dobrovolski, Vladislav Volkov and Viktor Parsayev. They dock with *Salyut 1* and make a stay of more than three weeks; but all three die during the landing phase of their mission.

June 11–August 4 The first flight by a lightplane from equator to equator via the North Pole is made by U.K. airwoman Sheila Scott flying a Piper Aztec D.

July 26–August 7 The U.S. achieves its fourth Moon landing with the *Apollo 15* mission. It is distinguished by the first use of the Lunar Roving Vehicle.

August 5 The U.K. Civil Aviation Act 1971 bill is approved, establishing the Civil Aviation Authority (CAA) and British Airways Board.

October 4 The Soviet Union announces that its *Lunokhod 1* lunar roving vehicle has ended its useful life.

October 10 Derived from Misrair, then assuming the name United Arab Airlines under President Nasser, Egypt's national airline becomes Egyptair on the above date.

October 11 The Soviet Union's orbiting space laboratory *Salyut 1* is destroyed as it re-enters the Earth's atmosphere after its mission had been terminated.

November 2 The first U.S. Defense Satellite Communications System Phase II satellites, or DSCS IIs, enter geosynchronous orbits.

November 23 Carried by an Aero Spacelines Super Guppy operated by Aeromaritime, the first set of Airbus A300B wings is delivered from Hawker Siddeley's Chester Factory to Toulouse, France.

December 6 The Spanish Government states that the nation's aircraft industry is to participate in the Airbus A300 programme.

December 13 A new Soviet deep space tracking and research ship, the *Kosmonavt Yuri Gagarin*, sails from Odessa on its maiden voyage.

January 4 Bangladesh Biman is formed as the national airline of the state of Bangladesh, formerly known as East Pakistan.

March 8 The Goodyear non-rigid airship *Europa*, which has been assembled in the U.K., makes its first flight from Cardington, Bedfordshire.

March 27 The Soviet Union's interplanetary probe *Venera 8* is launched towards Venus. An instrument capsule is landed successfully on the surface of the planet on July 22, 1972, transmitting data for a period of 50 minutes.

April 1 The British Airways Board combines the activities of BEA and BOAC under the title of British Airways.

The U.K. Civil Aviation Authority (CAA), the nation's first independent body for regulating civil aviation and providing air traffic control and navigation service, begins its functions.

April 16–27 NASA's *Apollo 16* mission, and the fifth Moon landing, is successfully carried out. Crewed by Lt. Col. Charles Duke, Lt. Cmdr. Thomas Mattingly and Capt. John Young, the Moon is used for astronomical purposes for the first time.

April 25 A Schleicher ASW 12 flown by Hans Gross (Germany) establishes a new world distance record for single-seat sailplanes of 907.7 miles (1,460.8km).

April 29 A specially-equipped McDonnell Douglas F-4 Phantom II becomes the first aircraft to be flown in the U.S. with a fly-by-wire control system.

May 10 India and the U.S.S.R. sign a development agreement under which the Soviet Union will launch India's first nationally-designed and built satellite.

The prototype of the Fairchild A-10A, one of the two contenders for the U.S.A.F.'s AX close-support requirement, makes its first flight.

May 26 At a summit meeting in Moscow, President Nixon and Leonid Brezhnev sign the first SALT agreement.

Cessna Aircraft Corporation announces completion of the company's 100,000th aircraft, the first company in the world to achieve such a production figure.

June 21 Jean Boulet flies an Aérospatiale Lama helicopter to a world record height of 40,820ft (12,442m).

July 23 The first U.S. Earth Resources Technology Satellite, or ERTS A, is launched. It is later renamed *Landsat 1*.

July 26 NASA announces that Rockwell International Corporation has been selected to build the Space Shuttle Orbiter, awarding the company an initial $450 million to cover the first two years of development.

1975 Aérospatiale/BAC Concorde

July 27 The first flight is made by the first pre-production McDonnell Douglas F-15A Eagle fighter (71-0280) from Edwards AFB, California.

August 28 H.R.H. Prince William of Gloucester and his passenger are killed in a flying accident at the beginning of a Goodyear Trophy Race in the U.K.

September 22 Receipt by the Boeing Company of an order for 14 Model 727s from Delta Air Lines brings total sales for this aircraft to 1,000. It is the first jetliner to attain such a sales figure.

September 29 The People's Republic of China and Japan sign a peace treaty, officially ending a state of war that had started 35 years earlier.

October 1 Malaysian Airline System (Sistem Penerbangan Malaysia Berhad), which had been established as the government-owned national airline during April 1971, begins scheduled operations.

October 20 The first flight is made at Toulouse-Blagnac of the first Airbus A300B1 (F-WUAB), piloted by Max Fischl.

December 7–19 NASA's successful *Apollo 17* mission is the last of the Moon landings. It, like those that preceded it, makes use of a Lunar Roving Vehicle, and a 75-hour stay on the lunar surface is the longest of the Apollo missions.

December 23 The Hertfordshire Pedal Aeronauts (HPA) Toucan man-powered aircraft makes a first flight of 2,100ft (640m) at Radlett. It is the first to have a two-man crew/power unit.

1973

January 7 The world's first hot-air airship (G-BAMK), developed in the U.K. by Cameron Balloons of Bristol, makes its successful first flight.

January 15 President Nixon orders a halt to air strikes and all other offensive military action against North Vietnam.

January 24 An agreement to end the war in Vietnam is initialled in Paris. It calls for a cease-fire at 23.59 hrs GMT on January 27.

February 23 The Aérospatiale/BAC Concorde 002 flies non-stop from Toulouse to Iceland and return. This represents a greater distance than the guaranteed entry-into-service range.

April 13 A deep-space tracking antenna with a diameter of 210ft (64m) is commissioned at Tidbinbilla, Australia.

May 14 The last Saturn V booster is used to launch NASA's *Skylab 1* Orbital Workshop into Earth orbit. Air pressure causes damage to a micrometeoroid shield immediately after lift-off.

May 20 Because of a 50-mile (80m) fishing limit dispute with U.K., the government of Iceland bans R.A.F. use of the NATO base at Keflavik.

May 22 Aero Perú (Empresa de Transporte Aéreo del Perú) is formed as the Government-owned national airline.

May 25 NASA's *Skylab 2* is launched into orbit to rendezvous with *Skylab 1*. Astronauts Charles Conrad, Joseph Kerwin and Paul Weitz are able to effect repairs to *Skylab 1* during several EVAs. Total mission time is 28 days 49 mins.

May 30 The first production SEPECAT Jaguar GR.Mk 1 for R.A.F. Strike Command is delivered to R.A.F. Lossiemouth, Morayshire.

June 3 The 30th Paris Air Show closes on a tragic note with the loss during a flying display of the second pre-production Tupolev Tu-144 SST, killing all six crew members.

June 26 A Pan American Boeing 747 carrying 220 passengers makes a completely uneventful fully-automatic landing at London Heathrow. This is made because storm damage to the flight-deck windscreen had completely cut off all forward view.

July 25 A. Fedotov, flying the Mikoyan Ye-266 in the Soviet Union, establishes a new world altitude record of 118,898ft (36,240m).

August 14 The U.S.A.F. ends its bombing attacks on Cambodia, terminating more than nine years of U.S. air combat in South-East Asia.

September 24 A Memorandum of Understanding is concluded between NASA and ESRO (European Space Research Organization). As a result, ESRO is given responsibility for design and construction of the Spacelab to be used in conjunction with NASA's Space Shuttle.

September 27–29 The Soviet Union's *Soyuz 12* mission carries cosmonauts Vasily Lazarev and Oleg Makarov into Earth orbit. This is the first Soyuz mission since the tragic loss of the *Soyuz 11* crew (q.v. June 6, 1971), and is the first flight of an improved *Soyuz* vehicle intended to serve as an Earth–space ferry to the Salyut space workshops.

October 6 A massive air strike by the Egyptian Air Force against Israeli artillery and command positions marks the beginning of the October or Yom Kippur war.

October 6–8 Israeli air counter-attack against Egypt's air and ground forces is frustrated by large-scale use of Soviet-made and effective SAMs.

October 21 At Linz, Austria, the Militky MB-EI (Militky Brditschka Electric 1) becomes the first electrically-powered manned aircraft to fly. A specially modified Brditschka HB-3 sailplane, it has a Bosch electric motor driven by rechargeable batteries.

1978 ACES II ejection seat

October 22 The first cease-fire is negotiated in the Yom Kippur war but fighting flares up again on the following day.

October 24 The second cease-fire of the Yom Kippur war is negotiated but only slowly comes into effect.

October 25 Tom Sage of the U.K. Cameron Balloon company establishes a hot-air balloon duration record of 5 hrs 45 mins.

November 16–February 8 NASA's *Skylab 4* is launched to rendezvous with *Skylab 1*, carrying astronauts Gerald Carr, Edward Gibson and William Pogue. This is the final Skylab mission and when the astronauts land they have completed a record 84 days 1 hr 15 mins in space.

December 3 The unmanned U.S. *Pioneer 10* is the first spacecraft to near Jupiter.

1974

January 1 Sikorsky S-61N helicopters operated by Bristow Helicopters mount a rescue operation, evacuating the 50-man crew of North Sea drilling platform *Transocean 3* shortly before it overturns.

January 4 Teledyne Ryan rolls out two YQM-98A RPV long-endurance reconnaissance prototypes. Built for the U.S.A.F.'s *Compass Cope* programme, they are designed to take off from and land on normal runways.

February 2 The first flight is made by the first General Dynamics YF-16 lightweight fighter prototype (72-01567) at Edwards AFB,

California. The same aircraft had made a brief unofficial first flight on January 20, when it lifted off during high-speed taxi tests.

February 18 U.S. Army reservist Col. Thomas Gatch lifts off from Pennsylvania in an attempt to make a North Atlantic balloon crossing. (q.v. February 21, 1974)

February 21 The distinctive balloon of Col. Gatch, comprising ten small balloons supporting a sealed and pressurized gondola, is reported by a merchant ship some 1,000 miles (1600km) west of the Canary Islands, but is never seen again.

March 3 To date the world's worst air disaster involving a single aircraft occurs soon after a THY Turkish Airlines McDonnell Douglas DC-10 takes off from Orly Airport. All 346 people on board are killed, and subsequent investigation shows that the failure of a cargo door had caused decompression, resulting in loss of control.

March 8 Charles de Gaulle Airport at Roissy-en-France, 15.5 miles (25km) from the centre of Paris and Europe's newest international airport, is officially opened by the French Prime Minister.

April 10 A Martin Marietta Titan III-D launches an additional *Big Bird* reconnaissance satellite into Earth orbit from Vandenberg AFB, California.

April 13 At Kennedy Space Center a Thor-Delta launcher is used to put the first of two *Westar* domestic comsats into geostationary orbit.

April 23 Bell Helicopters announce the delivery of the company's 20,000th helicopter. Of this total, some 80 per cent have been delivered since the beginning of 1964.

May 23 Europe's first wide-body jetliner, an Airbus A300B2 of Air France, makes its inaugural revenue flight on the airline's Paris–London route.

June 9 The first of Northrop's two YF-17 lightweight fighter prototypes (72-01569) makes its first flight. They are built for the U.S.A.F. LWF programme and are to be flown in competition against the General Dynamics YF-16s. (q.v. February 2, 1974)

August 14 The Panavia 200 MRCA prototype (D-9591) makes its first flight at Manching, West Germany, piloted by BAC's Paul Millet.

August 19 The Cameron balloon *Gerard A. Heineken* is flown for the first time at Bristol, Somerset. Then the world's largest hot-air balloon with a volume of 500,000cu ft (14,158m³), its two-tier basket could accommodate a total of 12 passengers.

August 26 The death is announced of Charles Lindbergh, one of the best known pilots in aviation history. His solo west-east crossing

of the North Atlantic, 47 years earlier, had captured the imagination and interest of the world.

August 30 Launch of the first Dutch satellite *ANS*.

August 31 The Apollo command module for the 1975 U.S./U.S.S.R. space flight is delivered to Kennedy Space Center by a Lockheed C-5A Galaxy.

October 17 The first flight is made at Stratford, Connecticut of the first of three Sikorsky YUH-60A prototypes (21650). This is a utility transport helicopter that has been designed to meet the U.S. Army's UTTAS (Utility Tactical Transport Aircraft System) requirement, to be flown in evaluation against Boeing Vertol YUH-61A contenders.

November 15 Launch of the first Spanish satellite *INTASAT*.

December 2–8 The Soviet Union places *Soyuz 16* into Earth orbit for a final rehearsal of the ASTP (Apollo-Soyuz Test Project) planned for 1975.

December 18 *Symphonie A*, Europe's first communications satellite, is launched into geostationary orbit by a Delta vehicle from Cape Kennedy.

December 23 The first flight is made by the first Rockwell International B-l prototype (71-40158) at Palmdale, California.

1975

January 14 It is announced in Washington that the U.S.A.F. has selected the General Dynamics YF-16 as the winner of its LWF (lightweight fighter) programme.

February 1 During a 16-day period that ended on this date, all eight world time-to-height records are captured by the McDonnell Douglas F-15 Eagle, named 'Streak Eagle'. The final record set a time of 3 mins 27.8 secs from standstill on a runway to a height of 98,425ft (30,000m).

February 22 First flight of the Soviet Su-25 *Frogfoot* subsonic close-air support aircraft, piloted by Vladimir Ilyushin. (q.v. February 4, 1981)

May 30 The European Space Agency (ESA) is founded.

June 3 The first flight is made by the first prototype Mitsubishi FS-T2-KAI, a single-seat supersonic close-support fighter developed from the T-2 jet trainer. Required to replace the JASDF's F-86F Sabres, it becomes designated F-l when it enters service.

June 8 The Soviet Union's *Venera 9* interplanetary 250 probe is launched towards Venus. This is very successful and later becomes the first artificial satellite of Venus. The data capsule which it ejects makes a successful landing on the planet's surface, its 53 minutes of transmission including TV pictures.

June 22 A new world speed record for women is established in the Soviet Union by Svetlana Savitskaya, flying a Mikoyan Ye-133 at a speed of 1,667.42mph (2,683.44km/h).

July 15–24 Combined U.S./U.S.S.R. space mission, during which the Soviet Union's *Soyuz 19* spacecraft and the U.S. Apollo ASTP (Apollo-Soyuz Test Project) dock together in Earth orbit for crew exchanges and combined experiments.

August 20 NASA's interplanetary probe *Viking 1* is launched. It subsequently places a landing module on Mars which transmits the first pictures of the planet's surface.

September 1 The fourth production Aérospatiale/BAC Concorde becomes the first aircraft to make two return transatlantic flights (London–Gander–London) or four transatlantic crossings in a single day.

September 16 The first flight of the Soviet Mikoyan MiG-31 *Foxhound* long-range interceptor.

September 30 A test flight is made by the first of two Hughes Model 77 (YAH-64) prototypes (22248). The YAH-64 is designed to meet the U.S. Army's Armed Attack Helicopter (AAH) requirement, and for fly-off evaluation against the Bell YAH-63.

November 17 The Soviet Union launches the unmanned *Soyuz 20* to conduct experiments in the resupply of Salyut space stations.

December 6 Carrying airmail between Moscow and Alma Ata, the Soviet Union's Tupolev Tu-144 SST makes the first airmail flight by a supersonic airliner.

1976

January 21 The world's first passenger services by a supersonic airliner are made, with Concorde SSTs of British Airways and Air France taking off simultaneously for Bahrain and Rio de Janeiro.

May 24 Air France and British Airways begin transatlantic Concorde passenger services from Paris and London, respectively, to Washington's Dulles International Airport.

June 22 The Soviet Union launches into Earth orbit the unmanned *Salyut 5* space station.

July 1 Clive Canning arrives in the U.K. after a solo flight from Australia in a homebuilt Thorp T-18 Tiger. This is the first Australia–England flight made in an aircraft of amateur construction

July 3 It is reported that in an Israeli commando assault on Entebbe airport on this date, the Israelis destroyed four MiG-17s and seven MiG-21s.

July 6 The Soviet Union launches *Soyuz 21* to dock with *Salyut 5* in orbit. Cosmonauts Boris Volynov and Vitali Zholobov carry out a 49 day 5 hr 24 min space mission.

July 28 Flying a Lockheed SR-71A strategic reconnaissance aircraft, Capt. E.W. Joersz and Maj. G.T. Morgan Jr., U.S.A.F., establish a new world speed record of 2,193.17mph (3,529.56km/h).

December 22 The prototype of the Soviet Union's Ilyushin Il-86 wide-body jetliner (CCCP-86000) makes its first flight from the old Moscow Central Airport of Khodinka, piloted by Hero of the Soviet Union A. Kuznetsov.

December 23 The Sikorsky S-70 (UH-60A) is declared winner of the U.S. Army's UTTAS competition for a primary combat assault helicopter.

1977

January 21 Bell makes the first tie-down test of the Model 301 (XV-15) tilt-rotor research aircraft.

February 17 Beech Aircraft Corporation completes production flight testing of its 10,000th Model 35 Bonanza.

February 18 The first flight of the Boeing 747 Space Shuttle carrier, with the Space Shuttle *Enterprise* mounted above the fuselage, is successfully made at NASA's Dryden Flight Research Center. In this test, and the five that are planned to follow, the *Enterprise* is unmanned.

March 24 The first operational Boeing E-3A AWACS aircraft is delivered to the U.S.A.F.'s 552nd Airborne Warning and Control Wing at Tinker AFB, Oklahoma.

March 27 The world's greatest air tragedy to date (583 fatalities) occurs when Pan Am and KLM Boeing 747s collide on the runway at Santa Cruz Airport, Tenerife.

May 3 The first of two Bell XV-15 tilt-rotor research aircraft (702) makes its first hovering flight.

May 19 The Soviet Union's *Cosmos 909* satellite is launched to serve as the target for a space interceptor satellite.

May 20 First flight of the Soviet Sukhoi Su-27 *Flanker* long-range fighter, piloted by Vladimir Ilyushin. (q.v. January 7, 1987)

June 13 President Carter gives his approval to the U.S. CAB's recommendation that Laker Airways should be allowed to operate a Skytrain service between London and New York for a one-year trial period.

June 17 The Soviet Union's *Cosmos 918* satellite is launched and intercepts the *Cosmos 909* target. (q.v. May 19)

June 30 President Carter announces cancellation of the Rockwell International B-1 supersonic strategic bomber programme: the U.S. is thus expected to rely on cruise missiles for strategic attack.

August 12 The U.S. Space Shuttle *Enterprise* makes its first free gliding flight following launch from the Boeing 747 Shuttle Carrier aircraft at a height of 22,800ft (6,950m).

August 20 NASA launches the unmanned spacecraft *Voyager 2*, which flies past Jupiter in July 1979 then continues via Saturn. Having passed Saturn, it is scheduled to reach Uranus in 1986.

August 23 *Gossamer Condor*, designed under the leadership of Dr. Paul MacCready in the U.S., and piloted by racing cyclist Bryan Allen, wins the £50,000 Kremer prize for the first 1-mile (1.6km) figure-of-eight flight by a man-powered aircraft.

August 31 In the Soviet Union, Alexander Fedotov, flying the Mikoyan Ye-266M, establishes a new world altitude record for air-breathing aircraft of 123,524ft (37,650m).

September 26 Six years after making initial proposals, Laker Airways inaugurates its London–New York Skytrain service. Almost immediately, six scheduled airlines introduce low-cost transatlantic fares.

October 6 First flight of the Soviet 9-01 prototype to the Mikoyan MiG-29 *Fulcrum* fighter, piloted by Alexander Fedotov.

November 22 After seemingly endless delays, Air France and British Airways inaugurate Concorde services to New York.

November 23 Launch of the first European weather satellite *Meteosat*.

December 1 First flight of the first of two Lockheed XST *Have Blue* stealth aircraft technology demonstrators at Groom Lake, Nevada. These assisted in the development of the F-117A stealth fighter. They are lost in 1978 and 1979.

December 4 British Airways, in conjunction with Singapore Airlines, begins Concorde services from Bahrain to Singapore.

December 14 First flight of the Soviet Mil Mi-26 *Halo* very heavy helicopter, the world's largest production helicopter, featuring an 8-blade main rotor.

1978

Introduction of the McDonnell Douglas Advanced Concept Ejection Seat II, also known as ACES II. (Subsequently used in the F-15, F-16, B-1B, B-2, A-10 and F-117A, it had saved over 200 lives by 1995, including nine ejections during the Gulf War.)

January 1 The assets and business of British Aircraft Corporation, Hawker Siddeley Aviation, Hawker Siddeley Dynamics and Scottish Aviation are transferred to British Aerospace. The latter corporation had been established by U.K. Government Act on April

29, 1977 and became technically the owner of the companies named above, although they had continued to trade under their original titles until this date.

January 10 The Soviet Union's *Soyuz 27* is launched to dock with *Salyut 6/Soyuz 26* in Earth orbit, its cosmonauts carrying mail and supplies to record the first mail delivery in space.

January 20 The Soviet Union's unmanned space ferry *Progress 1* is launched, carrying supplies to and docking automatically with *Salyut 6*.

February 22 The first Global Positioning System satellite is launched into Earth orbit.

March 2 Vladimir Remek is carried as a crew member aboard *Soyuz 28*, thus becoming the first Czechoslovakian to take part in a space mission.

March 10 The first flight is made at Istres of the first Dassault Mirage 2000 prototype, a single-seat interceptor and air superiority fighter that was selected in 1975 as the primary combat aircraft for service with the French Air Force from the mid-1980s.

April 19 ICAO delegates meeting in Montreal vote in favour of the U.S.-developed Time Reference Scanning Beam microwave landing system, selecting it for introduction as the standard international landing system by 1995.

May 9 David Cook, flying a Revell VJ-23-powered hang-glider, records the first crossing of the English Channel by such an aircraft.

May 21 Some four years later than planned, largely because of action by protesters, Tokyo's new Narita International Airport becomes operational.

June 6 It is reported that Aeroflot's Tu-144 services between Moscow and Alma Ata have been suspended because of excessive fuel consumption.

June 27 The Soviet Union launches *Soyuz 30* to dock with *Salyut 6*. In an operation similar to that of the *Soyuz 28* mission, Miroslaw Giermaszewski becomes the first Pole to take part in a space mission.

August 12–17 A balloon duration record of 137 hrs 5 mins 50 secs, a record distance of 3,107.62 miles (5,001.22km), and the first transatlantic crossing by a gas balloon, is recorded by *Double Eagle II*, crewed by Ben L. Abruzzo, Maxie L. Anderson and Larry M. Newman.

August 20 The first flight is made by the British Aerospace Sea Harrier FRS.Mk 1 (XZ450) from the company's airfield at Dunsfold, Surrey.

August 26 The Soviet Union launches *Soyuz 31*, crewed by Valery Bykovsky and the East German Sigmund Jahn. They return to earth in *Soyuz 29*, having previously docked with the *Salyut 6* space station.

October 2 Aeroflot begins route-proving trials with the Ilyushin Il-86 on its Moscow–Mineralnye Vody route.

November 9 The McDonnell Douglas YAV-8B Advanced Harrier prototype (158394) makes its first flight, a development of the British Aerospace Harrier to give increased weapons payload/combat radius.

November 18 The first flight is made by the McDonnell Douglas F/A-18 Hornet prototype (160775), a single-seat carrier-based fighter developed jointly by McDonnell Douglas and Northrop from the latter company's YF-17 prototype (that had taken part in the U.S.A.F.'s LWF programme).

December 19 Britons David Williams and Fred To fly *Solar One*, the world's first solar-powered aircraft.

December 19 First flight of the Soviet Beriev A-50 *Mainstay* airborne early warning and control aircraft, based on an Ilyushin Il-76MD airframe. Pilot is Vladimir Demyanovsky.

1979

January 1 Boeing E-3A Sentry AWACS aircraft of the U.S.A.F.'s 552nd Airborne Warning and Control Wing begin to assume a role in U.S. air defence.

January 6 The first General Dynamics F-16A single-seat lightweight air combat fighter is officially handed over to the U.S.A.F.'s 388th Tactical Fighter Wing at Hill AFB, Utah.

February 3 An unusual first flight is recorded at Cardington, Bedfordshire, by the Aerospace Developments AD 500 non-rigid airship (C-BECE). This has an overall length of 164ft (50m).

February 27 Production of the McDonnell Douglas A-4 Skyhawk ends after 26 years with the delivery of the 2,960th and last (an A-4M) to the U.S.M.C.'s Marine Attack Squadron VMA-331.

April 15 The first flight is made by the Dassault Mirage 50 prototype, a multi-mission fighter retaining the basic airframe of the Mirage III/5 series but incorporating the higher-rated SNECMA Atar 9K-50 turbojet.

April 20 The 16th and last production Concorde makes its first flight.

June 5 The *Chrysalis* man-powered biplane built at the Massachusetts Institute of Technology makes its first flight. When dismantled in September 1979, 345 flights have been made by 44 different pilots.

June 12 The *Gossamer Albatross*, designed and built under the leadership of Dr. Paul MacCready, wins the £100,000 Kremer prize for a first crossing of the English Channel by a man-powered aircraft.

July 11 The U.S. *Skylab* space station re-enters Earth's atmosphere and breaks up, pieces falling on Australia and in the Indian Ocean.

September 19 The Royal Navy's first Sea Harrier squadron, No. 700A, is commissioned at R.N.A.S. Yeovilton, Somerset. No. 700A later becomes the shore-based No. 899 H.Q. Squadron. Front line Sea Harrier units become Nos. 800, 801 and 802 Squadrons.

October 15 The 4450th Tactical Group, U.S.A.F., is formed to receive F-117A stealth fighters. (q.v. August 23, 1982)

1980

March 28 Gates Learjet announces that it has delivered its 1,000th Learjet.

April 18 The name Air Zimbabwe is adopted from the former temporary Air Zimbabwe Rhodesia. It had been formed originally as Air Rhodesia in September 1967.

April 24 An attempt to rescue American hostages held in Iran is initiated as Operation *Evening Light*. Sikorsky RH-53 Sea Stallion helicopters from U.S.S. *Nimitz* are among aircraft used, but the rescue fails as accidents at a desert landing area bring an end to the mission.

June 5 The Soviet Union's first manned *Soyuz T* capsule, incorporating an automatic docking system, is launched into Earth orbit.

July 18 The Indian Space Research Organization (ISRO) successfully launches into Earth orbit the *Rohini RS-1* test satellite, designed primarily to evaluate the efficiency of the SLV-3 launch vehicle.

August 7 The MacCready *Gossamer Penguin* makes its first straight (no turns) solar-powered flight of about 2 miles (3 km), piloted by Janice Brown.

September 19 Fighting breaks out between the nations of Iran and Iraq, with extensive use of air power being made.

September 22 The Royal Navy's last conventional aircraft carrier, H.M.S. *Ark Royal*, sails from Plymouth en route to the scrapyard.

October 2 A Westland Sea King helicopter is used in the rescue of 22 crew and passengers from the Swedish freighter *Finneagle* on fire at sea. The operation is carried out in 80-mph (129km/h) winds with very high sea conditions, and with a crew of four and a doctor, a total of 27 persons is carried by the Sea King on its return flight to Kirkwall, Orkney Islands.

October 11 Soviet cosmonauts Valeri Ryumin and Leonid Popov land successfully in *Soyuz 37* after spending 185 days in space on board the *Salyut 6* orbiting laboratory. During that period they have received visits and supplies from three manned spacecraft, and supplies and equipment from three unmanned Progress cargo spacecraft.

October 11–15 The Goodyear airship *Europa* is used for pollution monitoring in the Gulf of Genoa as part of a Mediterranean Pollution Monitoring Research Programme.

November 6 First battery-powered flight test is made at Shafter, California, of the *Solar Challenger* designed under the leadership of Dr. Paul MacCready.

November 9 The last revenue flight of a de Havilland Comet 4C (G-BDIW) is made from London Gatwick, a special flight for air enthusiasts and recalling the first flight more than 30 years earlier.

November 11 NASA's *Voyager 1* spacecraft flies past Saturn's largest moon, Titan, at a distance of about 2,796 miles (4,500km). It subsequently passes below Saturn's rings before travelling on out of the solar system.

November 18–21 British airwoman Judith Chisholm, flying a Cessna Turbo Centurion, establishes a new woman's solo flight record between England and Australia of 3 days and 13 hrs.

November 20 The MacCready *Solar Challenger* makes its first short-duration test flight solely on solar power.

December 3 Judith Chisholm (q.v. November 18) lands at London Heathrow after completing her solo round-the-world flight in 15 days 22 mins 30 secs and thus virtually halving the previous time set by Sheila Scott.

December 5 Piloted by Janice Brown, Dr. Paul MacCready's *Solar Challenger* records a flight under solar power only of 1 hr 32 mins.

December 6 The MacCready *Solar Challenger* is flown for a distance of 18 miles (29km) between Tucson and Phoenix, Arizona, the flight being terminated by a heavy rainstorm.

1981

January 1 In accordance with U.K. Government plans to return British Aerospace to private ownership, British Aerospace Ltd. is vested with all assets, liabilities and obligations of the nationalized corporation. It is then re-registered as British Aerospace Public Limited Company.

January 15 Operating in a 80-mph (129km/h) blizzard, Bell 212s of Bristow Helicopters, a Sikorsky S-61N of British Airways Helicopters and Westland Sea Kings of the Royal Norwegian Air Force combine efforts to rescue nine men from a sinking vessel some 115 miles (185km) north-east of the Shetlands.

January 18 A Bell Model 222 light commercial helicopter delivered to Omniflight Helicopters is the company's 25,000th production helicopter.

January 26 Pan American flies its last service with the Boeing Model 707-320C: Model 707s had been operated by the airline for just over 22 years.

The Soviet Union's *Progress 12* unmanned cargo spacecraft docks with and automatically refuels *Salyut 6* in Earth orbit. Two days later, *Progress 12* is used to raise the space station's orbit.

January 30 British Airways makes a record 96 automatic landings at London Heathrow on a day when fog has virtually closed the airport to other airlines, with an RVR of 410–492ft (125–150m) throughout the day.

February 4 The first Sukhoi Su-25 unit becomes operational as the 200th Independent Attack Air Flight of the Soviet air force, formed with 12 aircraft at the Sital-chai base in Azerbaijan. (q.v. February 22, 1975)

February 12 U.S. balloonists Max Anderson and Don Ida lift off from Luxor, Egypt in the helium-filled balloon *Jules Verne*. Their round-the-world flight attempt is aborted two days later after travelling some 2,900 miles (4,667km) to a point east of New Delhi.

April 12 U.K. hot-air balloon manufacturer Thunder-Colt Balloons records the first flight of its new AS 80 hot-air airship.

NASA's Space Shuttle *Columbia* is successfully launched from Cape Kennedy on mission STS-1, under the power of its own rocket engines and two jettisonable boosters. It is crewed by John Young and Robert Crippen and makes 37 orbits. The flight lasts for 2 days 6 hrs 21 mins. (q.v. April 14, 1981)

April 14 After 37 orbits of the Earth, *Columbia* makes a controlled re-entry into the atmosphere before completing a near-perfect unpowered landing on the dry bed of Rogers Lake at Edwards AFB, California.

June 5 Flying a specially-prepared Rutan Long-EZ lightplane, Richard G. Rutan sets a world straight-line distance record in the FAI-class C-l-b. The distance of 4,563.7 miles (7,344.56km) is subsequently ratified by the FAI.

June 7 Eight Israeli Air Force F-16s, escorted by F-15s, attack the Osirak nuclear reactor near Baghdad, Iraq. As a result, the U. S. imposes a temporary embargo on the supply of further F-16s to Israel.

June 19 Launch of the French *Meteostat 2* weather satellite by Ariana LO 3 rocket booster from Kouron, French Guyana.

July 7 The MacCready *Solar Challenger* makes the first crossing of the English Channel by a solar-powered aircraft. The 5 hr 23 min (180-mile/290-km) flight from Cergy Pontaire, near Paris to Cranston Airfield, Kent is piloted by Steve Ptacek.

August 3 The Boeing Company attains a new production milestone with the delivery of its 4,000th jetliner, a 727-200 for Ansett Airlines of Australia.

August 25 The NASA *Voyager 2* spacecraft makes its closest approach to the planet Saturn, returning spectacular pictures of its moons and rings. Next rendezvous for *Voyager 2* is with Uranus in January 1986.

September 7 Edwin A. Link, inventor of the Link trainer, dies at the age of 77. His ground-based flight trainer was the first stepping-stone towards the sophisticated flight simulators now used for a major portion of all flight training.

September 20 The People's Republic of China launches three satellites into Earth orbit with a single booster rocket. It is the nation's first multiple launch.

September 22 An Ilyushin Il-86, captained by G. Volokhov, establishes for the Soviet Union a new world-class record for speed in a 2,000-km closed circuit, carrying payloads of 35,000 to 65,000kg, of 606.02mph (975.3km/h). Two days later the same aircraft/crew combination sets a new record over a 1,000-km closed circuit of 597.8mph (962km/h) carrying payloads from 30,000 to 80,000kg.

September 26 The first flight of the Boeing Model 767 is successfully completed at Paine Field, Everett. This 2 hr 4 min flight is made three days ahead of a target that was set in 1978.

September 30 The last de Havilland Comet airliner flight in the U.K. is made by the Srs 4C G-BOIX, flown by Dan-Air to East Fortune for the Royal Scottish Museum.

October 2 President Reagan announces that 100 Rockwell B-1B SAL (Strategic Air-launched cruise missile Launchers) are to be procured for the U.S.A.F.

October 6 The first flight is recorded of an Airbus A300 with a two-man Forward Facing Crew Cockpit (FFCC). The FFCC flight deck has advanced avionics and improved system automation, making it possible for a flight crew of two to operate this wide-body airliner.

October 9 Ascending from a site near Los Angeles, California, Fred Gorrell and John Shoecroft in the helium-filled balloon *Superchicken III* record the first non-stop trans-America flight in a balloon, landing in Georgia 55 hrs 25 mins after lift-off.

November 4 NASA's second flight by the Space Shuttle *Columbia* is aborted 31 seconds before lift-off due to a computer mismatch.

November 12 The NASA Space Shuttle *Columbia*, on mission STS-2, makes a successful lift-off from Kennedy Space Center with Joe Engle and Richard Truly as crew. Thirty-six orbits are performed, the mission lasting for 2 days 6hrs 13 mins. A fuel cell fault halved the expected 5-day mission.

November 13 Ben Abruzzo, Larry Newman, Ron Clarke and Rocky Aoki complete the first manned crossing of the Pacific by balloon. Carried in the helium-filled balloon *Double Eagle V*, their journey from Nagashima, Japan, ends in a crash-landing in severe weather some 170 miles (274km) north of San Francisco.

November 14 With its mission cut short because of a fuel cell failure, the Space Shuttle *Columbia* makes a successful landing at Rogers Lake, Edwards AFB, California.

November 24 Two Sikorsky S-61Ns of Bristow Helicopters, operating in winds of about 87mph (140km/h), rescue 48 oilmen from the production rig *Transworld 58* after it had been blown from its moorings.

November 25–26 Crewed by French balloonists Hélène Dorigny and Michael Arnould, the Cameron A-530 hot-air balloon *Semiramis* is flown from Ballina, Ireland, to St.-Christophe-en-Boucherie, France. This is later ratified by the FAI as a new hot-air balloon distance record of 717.5 miles (1,154.74km).

December 4 NASA accepts the first flight-standard ERNO Spacelab module at ERNO's Bremen factory.

December 5 Jerry Mullen takes off in an aircraft named *Phoenix*, used formerly by Jim Bede as the BD-2 *Love One*, to attempt a closed-circuit distance record for piston-engined aircraft in Class C-l-d. He lands on December 8 after 73 hrs 2 mins in the air, having flown a distance of 10,007.1 miles (16,104.9km), which considerably exceeds the previous world record.

December 19 First flight of the Soviet Tupolev Tu-160 *Blackjack* supersonic heavy bomber, initially intended to carry cruise missiles. (q.v. April 25, 1987)

1982

January 6 A Gulfstream III executive transport, operated by the U.S. National Distillers and Chemical Corporation, begins a round-the-world flight. Landing on January 10, the flight (from and to Teterboro, New Jersey) is completed in 47 hrs 39 mins, breaking three existing records and setting 10 new records in the appropriate FAI class.

January 27 Cessna Aircraft Company announce delivery of its 1,000th business jet, a Citation II.

February 19 The Boeing Model 757 makes its first flight at Renton, Washington. The successful 2 hr 30 min flight terminates at Paine Field, Everett, where it is to be based until cleared by the FAA for operation from the company's airfield at Seattle.

1982 Naval Sea Harrier and R.A.F. Harrier during the Falklands war

April 2 Argentine Forces invade the Falkland Islands and, on the following day, the island of South Georgia.

April 3 The United Nations Security Council passes Resolution 502, calling for the withdrawal of Argentine forces from the Falklands.

The first Airbus A310 (F-WZLH) makes a successful first flight of 3 hrs 15 mins at Toulouse, France.

The main elements of the British task force for operations against the Argentine forces on the Falklands sail from Portsmouth. These include the carriers H.M.S. *Hermes* and *Invincible*.

April 6 A new Sea Harrier squadron, No. 809, is formed at R.N.A.S. Yeovilton. Nos. 800, 801, 809 and 899 Sea Harrier squadrons carry out 2,376 sorties and complete 2,675 hrs 25 mins of operational flying during the Falklands conflict that follows.

April 7 The British Government declares a 200-mile (322km) exclusion zone around the Falkland Islands.

April 21 Two Westland Wessex helicopters of the British task force crash on South Georgia in bad weather. A third recovers the men of the SAS.

April 25 Aircraft attached to the British task force despatched to the Falkland Islands are in action for the first time. Lynx helicopters flying from the frigates H.M.S. *Alacrity* and *Antelope* attack the Argentine submarine *Santa Fe* off Grytviken harbour, South Georgia. Later that day, Sea Kings escorted by Lynx helicopters

land Royal Marines on South Georgia. The Marines subsequently recapture the island.

April 28 The British Government gives Argentina 48 hours warning that an air blockade is to be imposed over a 200-mile (322km) radius from the Falklands.

May 1 The first British air attack against Argentine positions on the Falkland Islands is made by a single Vulcan B2 operating from Ascension Island. It requires flight refuelling on both the outward and return flights. The Vulcan bombs Port Stanley airfield, and an attack on the same airfield is made immediately afterwards by nine Sea Harriers from H.M.S. *Hermes*. Three Sea Harriers also attack the airstrip at Goose Green. The Vulcan operation against Port Stanley from Ascension Island ranks then as the longest-ever operational sortie.

In the first Sea Harrier combat victory, an Argentine Mirage IIIEA is destroyed by a Sidewinder missile. Argentine losses on the same day include a second Mirage III and a Canberra bomber.

May 2 A Royal Navy ASW Sea King helicopter under fire from the Argentine patrol vessel *Alferez Sobral* reports its position to the task force. Soon afterwards the *Sobral* is severely damaged in an attack by two Lynx helicopters deploying Sea Skua missiles and an accompanying patrol vessel, the *Comodoro Somellera*, is sunk.

The Argentine Navy cruiser *General Belgrano* is sunk by the British nuclear-powered submarine *Conqueror*.

May 4 A Sea Harrier is lost during an attack on Port Stanley.

H.M.S. *Sheffield*, a Type 42 destroyer, has to be abandoned and later sinks after being hit by an Exocet missile launched from an Argentine Navy Dassault-Bréguet Super Étendard recently supplied from France.

May 5 Two British Airways L-1011 TriStars make safe touch-downs at London's Heathrow Airport in totally blind conditions. The landings are made with an absence of runway visual range and reference height measurements.

May 7 The British Government declares a 'safe zone' extending 12 miles (19.3km) from the Argentine coast.

Two Sea Harriers from H.M.S. *Invincible* are lost; it is believed they collided in poor visibility.

May 8 About 20 Harriers and Sea Harriers fly non-stop from R.N.A.S. Yeovilton, Somerset, to Ascension Island, air-refuelled several times during the 9-hour flight.

May 9 The Argentine vessel *Nawal*, shadowing the British task force, is attacked by two Sea Harriers. Its crew subsequently surrenders to a boarding party from H.M.S. *Hermes*.

May 13 The *Soyuz T-5* is launched successfully from Baikonur, carrying cosmonauts Anatoli Berezovoy and Valentin Lebedev. A successful link-up is made on May 14 with the Soviet Union's new orbiting laboratory, *Salyut 7*.

May 14 The British task force raids Pebble Island; three Argentine Skyhawk attack-bombers are lost in action.

India's combined communications and weather satellite, *Insat 1A*, becomes operational.

May 17 In what is believed to be the first launch of a satellite from an orbiting space station, the crew of *Salyut 7* place the amateur radio satellite *Iskra 2* in Earth orbit via an airlock in the space laboratory. (q.v. May 13, 1982)

May 21 Royal Marine Commandos and a Parachute Regiment battalion make a successful landing at Port San Carlos on the East Falklands. Royal Navy Sea Kings play a major role in this action; for example, a detachment of Sea King Mk. 4 Commando helicopters of No. 846 Squadron airlift more than 407 tons of stores and 520 troops on this day alone. The Type 21 frigate H.M.S. *Ardent* is lost after air attack. Nine Argentine aircraft are lost in action.

May 24 Following several hits by rockets and bombs launched from Argentine aircraft on the previous day, the frigate H.M.S. *Antelope* explodes and sinks. Seven Argentine aircraft are lost in action.

May 25 The Type 42 destroyer H.M.S. *Coventry* of the British task force is hit by bombs from Argentine Skyhawks and sinks following serious fire damage. In another attack, the container ship *Atlantic Conveyor* is hit by an Exocet missile launched from an Argentine Navy Super Étendard and is abandoned after serious fire damage. Twenty-four task force personnel lose their lives.

May 28 Goose Green and Darwin are retaken by British forces. Seventeen British soldiers are killed in the action.

June 3 An R.A.F. *Vulcan* is intercepted in Brazilian airspace and escorted to Rio de Janeiro by Brazilian F-5Es.

June 8 Argentine aircraft attack task-force ships at Bluff Cove. Fifty task-force personnel lose their lives. Eleven Argentine aircraft are lost in action.

June 12 H.M.S. *Glamorgan* is struck by a land-based Exocet fired from Port Stanley. Thirteen sailors are lost but the destroyer remains operational.

June 14 Argentine forces on the Falklands surrender. Argentine losses amount to more than 700 killed, five ships and well over 100 aircraft. British air losses total four Sea Harriers lost in accidents, two lost to ground fire, three Harrier GR Mk 3s lost to ground fire and helicopters. No Harrier/Sea Harrier has been lost in air-to-air combat.

July 27 Space Shuttle *Columbia* is launched on mission STS-4, its last proving flight. Crewed by Mattingly and Hartsfield, the mission lasts for 7 days 1 hr 10 mins and sees the first Shuttle landing on a concrete runway.

August 5 Australian Dick Smith begins the first solo helicopter flight around the world. (q.v. July 22, 1983)

August 23 The first of 59 Lockheed F-117A stealth fighters are delivered to the U.S.A.F. (last on July 12, 1990). Initial operational capability by the 4450th Test Squadron is in October of the following year.

September 30 The first round-the-world flight by helicopter is completed by H. Ross Perot Jr. and Jay W. Coburn in a Bell Model 206L LongRanger II named *The Spirit of Texas*. Begun on September 1, the crew made 29 landings in 23 different countries during the staged flight, with fuel also being taken on from S.S. *President McKinley* in the North Pacific. The calculated distance flown is 26,000 miles (41,850km). Modifications to the helicopter include the addition of a 151 U.S. gallon auxiliary fuel tank in the cabin, increasing the helicopter's range to 750 miles (1,207km). This also establishes an FAA world speed record for helicopters flying around the world of 35.4mph (56.97km/h).

November 4 Pan American Boeing 747SPs inaugurate services between Los Angeles (U.S.A.) and Sydney (Australia), a distance of 7,487 miles (12,049km). It is said by the airline to be the world's longest non-stop commercial route.

1982 F-117A stealth fighter

November 8 An R.A.F. Tornado GR.Mk 1 makes a non-stop two-way flight between England and Cyprus. Flight-refuelled by Victors and a Buccaneer, it is one of No. 9 Squadron's aircraft, the R.A.F.'s first operational Tornado squadron (since June 1, 1982).

November 11 Space Shuttle mission STS-5 using *Columbia* begins. Lasting 5 days 2 hrs 14 mins, it is the first operational flight, deploying *Anik-3*. Crew comprises Allen, Brand, Lenoir and Overmyer.

December 16 The Boeing AGM-86B air-launched cruise missile (ALCM) attains initial operational capability on Boeing B-52 Stratofortress bombers.

December 20 Launch of the first Defense Meteorological Satellite Program satellite.

December 21 With the disbanding of No. 44 Squadron, the R.A.F. finally gives up its last Avro Vulcan bombers. This leaves the R.A.F. with no operational bombers as such.

December 26 The prototype Antonov An-124 *Condor* flies for the first time. It is then the world's largest aircraft.

1983

February 17 When an Italian Air Force pilot ejects from his Aeritalia F-104S Starfighter, he becomes the 5,000th person to be saved using Martin-Baker ejection seats.

April 5 Space Shuttle mission STS-6 using *Challenger* begins after a long delay caused by leaks. It sees the first EVA from an Orbiter. Crew comprises Bobko, Musgrave, Peterson and Weitz.

April 26 A sum of £100,000 is given to the Royal Aeronautical Society by Henry Kremer to further promote the development of man-powered aircraft. Intended to encourage greater speeds, an initial award of £20,000 is offered by the Society for a man-powered flight of one mile in under three minutes.

May 14 The Hughes Flying Boat Exhibition, housing the H-4 Hercules *Spruce Goose*, is opened to the public at Long Beach, California.

May 22 A French Aviasud Sirocco makes the first flight across the Mediterranean by a microlight aircraft.

June 18 Space Shuttle mission STS-7 using *Challenger* begins. It lasts 6 days 2 hrs 24 mins. *Anik-C2* and *Palapa-B1* are deployed (Canadian and Indonesian satellites). Also sees the first satellite retrieval and the first American woman in space (Dr. Sally Ride, at 32 the youngest U.S. astronaut). Other crew members are Crippen, Fabian, Hauck and Thagard.

July 22 Australian Dick Smith completes the first solo flight around the world in a helicopter. The 35,258-mile (56,742-km)

journey was made in stages, with the Bell JetRanger III *Australian Explorer* accumulating an actual flying time of some 320 hrs.

August 19 Lockheed rolls out its 250th and last TriStar airliner at Palmdale, California.

August 30 Space Shuttle mission STS-8 begins, lasting 6 days 7 mins. Crewed by Bluford, Brandenstein, Gardner, Thornton and Truly, it is the first night launch and landing.

September Soviet *Soyuz T-10* launch ends with an explosion on the Tyuratam launch pad. The two crew fly to safety using the launch escape system.

September 6 It is acknowledged that a Soviet Air Force Sukhoi Su-15 interceptor is responsible for shooting down a Korean Air Lines Boeing Model 747, with the loss of 269 lives. The airliner had flown off-course, taking it over Sakhalin Island.

September 30 Roll-out of the first production McDonnell Douglas (Hughes) AH-64A Apache attack helicopter. IOC is achieved by the 6th Cavalry Regiment's 3rd Squadron in July 1986.

October 26 With a special Boeing 707 flight between New York and Paris, Pan American commemorates the 25th anniversary of 707 transatlantic services.

November 28 Space Shuttle mission STS-9/41-A begins *Spacelab 1* mission.

December 16 The Chiefs of Staff of the British, French, West German, Italian and Spanish air forces sign a preliminary design agreement for a Future European Fighter Aircraft. France withdraws in July 1985. (q.v. June 1986)

1984

January 12 The U.S. Marine Corps receives its first McDonnell Douglas/BAe AV-8B Harrier II.

February 3 Space Shuttle mission 41-B begins using *Challenger*, lasting 7 days 23 hrs 17 mins. *Palapa B2* and *Westar 6* satellites are lost. Bruce McCandless makes the first untethered EVA using the Martin Marietta Manned Manoeuvring Unit.

March 6 The British Airship Industrie's Skyship 600 makes its first flight at Cardington, Bedfordshire.

March 27 British Airways starts a thrice-weekly return service between London, Heathrow and Miami, using Concorde.

March 31 No. 50 Squadron, R.A.F., is disbanded at Waddington, Lincolnshire. This sees the Avro Vulcan finally out of service in all roles.

April 4 Space Shuttle mission 41-C begins using *Challenger*, lasting 6 days 23 hrs 40 mins. During the mission, the *Solar Maximum* satellite is retrieved, repaired and redeployed.

1983 H-4 entering the exhibition dome (courtesy Wrather Port Properties Ltd.)

May 15 The Aeritalia/Aermacchi/EMBRAER AMX close-support aircraft makes its first flight.

June 22 Voyager Aircraft Inc.'s *Voyager* flies for the first time, with Dick Rutan at the controls (30 mins). Designed by Rutan, it is expected to attempt a non-stop and unrefuelled flight around the world. The next test flight takes place on the 24th, lasting three hours. (q.v. December 14–23, 1986)

July 2 Escadron de Chasse (EC) 1/2 *Cigognes* at Dijon is the first squadron to become operational with the Dassault-Bréguet Mirage 2000.

July 25 Soviet cosmonaut Svetlana Savitskaya makes the first EVA 'spacewalk' by a woman, leaving the *Salyut 7/Soyuz T-10B/Soyuz T-12* complex for 3 hrs 35 mins 4 secs. She is also the first woman to fly twice in space.

August 30 Space Shuttle mission 41-D using *Discovery*, the 12th mission, begins. It lasts 6 days 56 mins and carries the first commercial payload specialist.

September 1984–March 1987 Frenchman Patrice Franceschi makes the first staged around-the-world flight in a microlight. Piloting an Aviasud Sirocco, some 27,960 miles (45,000km) are covered in a flying time of about 700 hrs.

September 14–18 Famous high-altitude parachute jumper, ex-U.S.A.F. Colonel Joe Kittinger, makes the first solo non-stop balloon flight across the North Atlantic. His 101,000cu ft (2,860m³) balloon *Rosie O'Grady* took off from Carbon, Maine, and lands at Savona, Italy.

October 2 *Soyuz T-10B* lands after setting a new space duration record of 237 days.

October 5 Space Shuttle mission 41-G begins using *Challenger*, following two cancelled missions. Lasting 8 days 5 hrs 23 mins, it has the first 7-person crew. Sally Ride becomes the first U.S. woman to fly into space twice. Kathryn Sullivan makes the first 'spacewalk' by a U.S. female astronaut. Also on board is Canadian Marc Garneau.

October 18 The first production Rockwell International B-1B strategic bomber makes its first flight.100 are on order.

November 3 As part of an international relief effort to help starving Ethiopia, the first of two R.A.F. Hercules transports arrive at Addis Ababa Airport. Seven-days-a-week flying begins on November 5, ending at the close of the year.

November 9 No. 849 Squadron, R.N.A.S. Culdrose, Cornwall, England, becomes the world's first helicopter airborne early-warning squadron.

November 20–22 Briton Julian Nott establishes a new world altitude record for manned pressurized balloons, taking *ULD 1* to a height of 17,767ft (5,415.4m). It also sets new duration and distance records for pressurized balloons, at 33 hrs 8 mins 42 secs and 1,485.98 miles (2,391.46km) respectively.

1985

A U.S. Boeing B-29 Superfortress of the 46th Reconnaissance Squadron based in Alaska is rediscovered virtually intact in Greenland, where it had been abandoned after running short of fuel during the return leg of a possibly-secret mission on February 21, 1947. Landed at night in snow on a frozen lake, the crew had been rescued by a C-54 transport a few days later.

January 27 Space Shuttle mission 51-C begins, using *Discovery*. Lasting 3 days 1 hr 33 mins, it is the first U.S. Department of Defense military mission, with the DoD flight engineer Payton on board. A signal-intelligence satellite is launched.

April 12 Space Shuttle mission 51-D begins, using *Discovery*. Lasting 6 days 23 hrs 56 mins, Senator Jake Garn is the Shuttle's first passenger/observer.

April 30 The first Harrier GR.Mk 5 development aircraft is flown by British Aerospace.

May 4 The second production Rockwell International B-1B bomber makes its first flight. It is delivered to the 96th Bomb Wing at Dyess Air Force Base, Texas on July 7. Initial Operational Capability is achieved in September 1986.

May 14 A prototype AIM-120A AMRAAM air-to-air missile is successfully test-fired at a QF-100 Super Sabre drone flying over White Sands, New Mexico.

1983 STS-7 Challenger

1984 Skyship 600 during trials

May 29 The Antonov An-124, then the world's largest aircraft, flies into Le Bourget to make its first public appearance at the Paris Air Show.

June 23 An Air India Boeing Model 747 is blown up by a bomb some 120 miles (193km) off Ireland. 321 people are killed.

August 2 West Germany, Italy and the U.K. sign an agreement for the development and production of the European Fighter Aircraft.

August 12 A Japan Air Lines Boeing 747SR crashes in mountains north of Tokyo. 520 persons are killed, the highest number of fatalities ever in a single aircraft to this date.

September 13 A U.S.A.F. McDonnell Douglas F-15 Eagle launches an anti-satellite missile from an altitude of about 40,000ft (12,190m). It destroys the inert *Solwind* research satellite in Earth orbit.

September 30 The new aircraft carrier, *Giuseppe Garibaldi*, is handed over to the Italian Navy. Although initially flying helicopters, its design allows for V/STOL jets of BAe Sea Harrier type.

October 3 Space Shuttle mission 51-J begins, using *Atlantis* for the first time. Lasts 4 days 1 hr 45 mins.

October 28 The Hazeltine Microwave Landing System installed at Westland Helicopters' Yeovil airfield is declared operational. It is the first in Europe.

October 30 Space Shuttle mission 61-A begins, paid for by West Germany and using *Columbia*. First eight-person crew, including Germans.

November 26 Space Shuttle mission 61-B begins, using *Atlantis*. Lasting over 6 days 22 hrs, Mexican (Neri) is among the seven crew.

December 5 The Soviet Union launches its first nuclear-powered aircraft carrier at the Nikolayev South yard, which is commissioned on January 21, 1991 and becomes *Admiral Kuznetsov* (formerly *Tbilisi*).

1986

January 28 Space Shuttle mission 51-L, using *Challenger*. The crew of seven are killed in an explosion 73 seconds after lift-off. Planned future Shuttle missions are cancelled while investigations take place.

March 13 The British Aerospace *Giotto* satellite, launched on July 2, 1986, intercepts Halley's Comet. It passes within 375 miles (605km) of the comet's nucleus.

March 26 The British Aerospace Terprom aircraft navigation system completes its technology demonstration trials. It has an accuracy of 150–300ft (45.7–91.4m) regardless of flight duration.

April 23 Scheduled passenger services over London landmarks are begun using an Airship Industries Skyship 500 airship.

May 10 A U.S.A.F. Boeing B-52H, flying from Carswell Air Force Base, Texas, for the first time carries a full load of 20 AGM-86B air-launched cruise missiles.

1984 R.A.F. Hercules in Ethiopia (courtesy CPL Geoff Whyham)

1985 Superfortress found in Greenland (courtesy Danish Embassy)

June Eurofighter Jagdflugzeug GmbH is formed in Munich to oversee the European Fighter Aircraft programme. (q.v. December 16, 1983)

July 1 Six Soviet Mikoyan MiG-29 *Fulcrum* fighters begin a courtesy visit to Rissala Air Base in Finland. It gives the West the first opportunity to see this new combat aircraft close-up.

July 4 The Dassault-Bréguet Rafale A experimental advanced combat aircraft makes its first flight, during which it achieves Mach 1.3+.

July 10 Dick Rutan and Jeana Yeager begin a five-day and 11,336.9-mile (18,245km) non-stop test flight in *Voyager*.

July 28 Seven American aircraft companies submit design proposals for the future AFT (Advanced Tactical Fighter). On October 31, the U.S.A.F. announces the Lockheed-Burbank YF-22A and Northrop YF-23A are to be developed.

August 11 The Westland Lynx demonstrator G-LYNX sets a new world speed record for helicopters by flying at 249.09mph (400.87km/h) over a 15/25km course. It uses the new BERP III main rotor blades for the record flight.

August 12 The first Japanese H-I rocket is launched, carrying an experimental geodetic satellite into orbit.

August 17 Boeing rolls out of its Seattle factory its 5,000th commercial jet airliner, a Model 737-300 for KLM.

August 28 Richard Meredith-Hardy begins a flight using a Mainair Gemini Flash 2 microlight that takes him in stages from London's Dockland to Cape Town, South Africa, in the British Trans-Africa Microlight Expedition. The journey of 10,700 miles (17,220km) takes 330 flying hours.

September 2 Henk and Evelyn Brink of the Netherlands make a record-breaking flight across the Atlantic in a Cameron R225 combined hot air/helium balloon, taking 50 hrs to fly from St. John's, Newfoundland, to a point near Amsterdam.

November 6 The worst civilian helicopter accident to date happens off Sumburgh, Shetland Islands, when 45 of the 47 persons on board a commercial Boeing 234 Chinook helicopter belonging to British International Helicopters are killed. (On May 10, 1977, 54 had been killed in an Israeli military Sikorsky Sea Stallion.)

December 8 First flight of the Russian Beriev A-40 ASW and SAR jet amphibian.

December 14–23 The *Voyager* composites trimaran aeroplane makes a successful non-stop and unrefuelled around-the-world flight, beginning and ending at Edwards Air Force Base. Crewed by Dick Rutan and Jeana Yeager, the actual time is 9 days 3 mins 44 secs. It establishes a world absolute distance record in a straight line and closed circuit for aeroplanes of 24,986.664 miles (40,212.139km).

1987

January 7 A Norwegian F-16 makes the first contact with a Soviet Sukhoi Su-27 fighter over the Barents Sea.

January 21 The Massachusetts Institute of Technology (MIT) *Michelob Light Eagle* human-powered aircraft is used to set world distance in a straight line, distance in a closed circuit and duration records for women at 4.255 miles (6.83km), 9.59 miles (15.44km) and 37 mins 38 secs respectively, piloted by American Lois McCallin.

January 22 The MIT *Michelob Light Eagle* sets a world distance record in a closed circuit for a human-powered aircraft of 36.452 miles (58.664km), piloted by Glenn Tremml.

February 5 The Soviet Union launches spacecraft TM2 with full television coverage. Col. Yuri Romanenko and Flight Engineer Alexander Laveikin (the 200th person in space) dock with the *Mir* space station on the 7th.

April 25 First two operational Soviet Tupolev Tu-160 *Blackjack* supersonic heavy cruise-missile bombers are delivered to the 184th Heavy Bomber Regiment of Guards at Priluki, Ukraine.

May 15 The Soviet Energia heavy rocket booster is first launched, capable of carrying a 100-ton payload.

July 2 The first transatlantic crossing by hot-air balloon begins from Sugar Loaf, Maine, U.S.A. Crewed by Richard Branson and Per Lindstrand, the *Virgin Atlantic Flyer* (at this time the world's largest hot-air balloon at 2,130.000cu ft/60,314.8m³) lands near Limavady, Northern Ireland the following day. Having entered a jetstream during its crossing, it achieved a computed maximum speed of 153mph (246km/h).

August 17 First flight of the first real prototype Russian Sukhoi Su-33 carrier-borne fighter and anti-shipping aircraft.

October 9 The first pre-production EH Industries EH 101 helicopter makes its maiden flight at Yeovil, England.

October 14 A de Havilland Canada DHC-7 Dash 7 of Brymon Airways makes the first passenger-carrying flight from Britain's new London City Airport. The destination is Paris, France.

October 26 The first revenue flight is made from London City Airport.

November 29 A Korean Air Lines Boeing Model 707 is destroyed in the air by a bomb reportedly planted by a North Korean woman. All 115 persons are killed.

December 8 The United States of America and the Soviet Union sign an Intermediate-range Nuclear Forces (INF) treaty. It is later ratified by Congress.

December 10 Two prisoners are helped to escape from the U.K.'s Gartree maximum security prison by a hijacked Bell Model 206L LongRanger helicopter.

December 21 Soviet cosmonauts Musa Manarov and Vladimir Titov are launched to the *Mir* space station. (q.v. November 11, 1988)

December 29 Soviet cosmonaut Yuri Romanenko returns to Earth in *Soyuz TM3* after a 326-day stay in space.

1988

February 25 India launches the Prithvi, a tactical surface-to-surface missile of its own development.

April 15 The first aeroplane fuelled by liquid hydrogen makes its maiden flight as the Soviet Tupolev Tu-155. It is basically a converted Tu-154 airliner.

June 1 Per Lindstrand pilots a 600,000cu ft (17,000m³) hot-air balloon to an altitude of 65,000ft (19,810m) over Texas, U.S.A., setting a new record.

June 7 The Soviet *Phobos* satellite is launched from Baikonur on a mission to Mars. A second satellite follows shortly after. They are to orbit Mars and land monitoring experiments onto the moon Phobos. The satellites carry equipment from 12 other nations and America's NASA Deep Space network helps with communications and other aspects of the mission.

June 28 First flight of the prototype Russian Sukhoi Su-35 advanced air-superiority fighter and attack aircraft.

July 1 The Chinese state airline, CAAC, becomes Air China.

July A cease-fire is proposed between Iraq and Iran.

August 1 In accordance with the INF Treaty, the first four Soviet SS-20 missiles with their warheads removed are blown up at the Sary Ozek base.

August 2 U.S. Defense Secretary Frank Carlucci inspects an example of the new Soviet Tupolev *Blackjack* bomber at Kubinka air base, near Moscow.

August 17 A Pakistan Air Force Lockheed C-130 Hercules crashes soon after take-off from Bakawalpur. Among the 30 killed is President Zia.

August 18 Indian industrialist Vijay Singhania flies from Biggin Hill, England, in the CFM Shadow microlight *l'Esprit D'Indian Post* in an attempt to fly to Bombay in 23 days.

August 28 Three Italian Air Force pilots are killed, together with 39 spectators when three Aermacchi MB-339PANs of the Italian Pattuglia Acrobatica Nazionale Frecce Tricolori aerobatic team collide during a display at the U.S.A.F.'s Ramstein Air Base in West Germany.

September 19 Israel launches its first satellite, the *Offeq 1*, from a Shavit booster.

September 28 The Soviet Ilyushin Il-96-300 wide-body airliner makes its maiden flight.

September 29 The U.S. Space Shuttle Orbiter programme resumes with the launch of STS-26, using *Discovery*. A Tracking and Data Relay Satellite System satellite is launched (TDRSS-C). The mission ends on October 3.

November Antonov displays its massive An-225 Mriya transport aircraft. Powered by six Lotarev D-18T turbofan engines, it weighs some 590 tons (600 tonnes) and is therefore nearly half as heavy again as the world's previously largest aircraft, the Antonov An-124. (q.v. December 21, 1988)

November 11 Soviet cosmonauts Musa Manarov and Vladimir Titov set a new space endurance record of 326 days. (q.v. December 21, 1987)

November 15 The Soviet Space Shuttle *Buran* is launched for the first time from the Baikonur Cosmodrome on a 3 hr 25 min unmanned flight. This was the third launch attempt and it uses an Energia booster rocket.

November 22 The Northrop B-2A advanced technology bomber is rolled out. B-2As will eventually complement B-1Bs as the U.S.A.F.'s main strategic bomber in the next decade.

December 9 Saab JAS 39 Gripen, a Swedish multi-role combat aircraft makes its first flight from Linköping. (q.v. June 1996)

December 21 First flight of the world's largest aircraft, the Ukrainian Antonov An-225 Mriya six-engined very heavy freighter. Only a single example is completed. Its first commercial flight takes place in May 1990, having earlier been used for the first time to transport the Russian *Buran* space shuttle on its back.

1989

The first hot-air airship with cargo-carrying capability flies as the Thunder & Colt AS 261. With a length of 156ft 10in (47.8m) and volume of 261,000cu ft (7,391m³), it is also (in 1989) the world's largest hot-air airship. Capable of carrying five crew and a 0.75-ton (0.76-tonne) suspended payload, it is used to air-lift an inflatable platform to the tree tops in the Brazilian rain forest to help with botanical investigations.

January 2 The first flight is recorded of the Soviet Tupolev Tu-204, from a Moscow airport.

January 8 The Soviet Union announces its intention to begin destroying its huge stockpile of chemical weapons. Western estimates for the size of the stockpile vary from 50 to 500,000 tons/tonnes. The U.S.A. is thought to have 30–42,000 tons/tonnes.

1989 Thunder & Colt AS 261 with inflatable platform (courtesy Thunder & Colt)

January 22 The Massachusetts Institute of Technology man-powered aircraft, *Michelob Light Eagle*, flies 36.452 miles (58.664km) under the pedal-power of Glenn Tremml.

March 15 Canadian Hilda Wallace becomes the oldest recorded person to gain a pilot's licence, at 80.3 years old.

April 11 Australian Eric Winton flies a Tyagarah Aerodrome to a new world altitude record of 29,999ft (9,144m).

May 28 First flight of the AIDC Ching-Kuo indigenous fighter and attack aircraft in Taiwan. Production deliveries began in January 1994, with initial operational capability achieved by No. 8 Squadron a year later.

June 8 Russian pilot Anatoli Kvochur ejects from his stricken Mikoyan MiG-29 at an altitude of just 400ft (122m) at the Paris Air Show after an engine cut-out. Having ensured that the nose-diving aircraft would miss the crowd, he ejects horizontally, just two seconds before impact.

July 17 First flight of the Northrop Grumman B-2A Spirit strategic stealth bomber, which had been under secret development since 1978. (q.v. December 11, 1993)

August 15 A McDonnell Douglas/BAe GR.Mk 5 Harrier II records the fastest climb to date, taking just 2 mins 6.63 secs to reach 39,370ft (12,000m) from a standing start.

August 21 A new world speed record for landplanes with piston engines is established by American Lyle Shelton, flying a modified

Grumman F8F Bearcat with a 3,800hp (2,834kW) Wright R-3350 radial engine. He achieves over 528mph (850km/h) over a 3-km course at Las Vegas.

November 1 A Sukhoi Su-27K (T10K-2, also known as Su-33) lands on the aircraft carrier *Tbilisi* (since renamed *Admiral Kuznetsov*), the first conventional fixed-wing aircraft to land on a Russian aircraft carrier. The same day an Su-25UTG shipborne trainer and Mikoyan MiG-29K fighter land on the carrier.

December A Bell Model 47B, accommodating Doug Daigle, Dave Meyer, Brian Watts and Ron Anderson, makes the longest helicopter hovering flight yet recorded, at 50 hrs 50 secs.

December 10 The California Polytechnic University's composites-built (balsa wood, carbon and plastics) *Da Vinci III* makes the first recognized and official flight by a human-powered helicopter, lasting 7.1 seconds and attaining a height of 8in (0.2m). Earlier flights, in November, had seen the helicopter lift off the ground, but very briefly.

December 20/21 First operational use of the U.S.A.F.'s Lockheed F-117A stealth fighter, when two aircraft release 2,000-lb laser-guided bombs on the Rio Hato barracks in Panama, under Operation *Just Cause*.

December 30 First flight of the Russian Sukhoi Su-30 *Flanker* two-seat long-range interceptor development of the Su-27.

1989–90

The Russian Tupolev Tu-160 *Blackjack* supersonic heavy strategic

bomber sets 44 speed, payload and height records, including a Class C-1-r record of 1,075mph (1,731km/h) over a 1,000-km closed circuit with a 66,140lb (30,000kg) payload.

1990

January 30 Northwest Airlines' flight attendant, Connie Walker, retires at the age of 70, after 42 years in the air.

February 25 No-smoking flights are compulsory for all U.S. airlines flying over North America.

March 10 The 6,000th Boeing jet airliner is delivered, a 767-200 to Britannia Airways.

March 29 First flight of the Russian Ilyushin Il-114 short-haul airliner.

April 13 First flight of the Russian Sukhoi Su-34 two-seat (side-by-side) tactical and theatre bomber, intended to replace the Su-24 and other combat types.

April 28 David Cook sets the current British altitude record for microlights, flying to 27,064ft (8,249m) over Aldeburgh. Suffolk.

May 1 First flight of the actual prototype McDonnell Douglas MD 520N NOTAR (no tail rotor) helicopter.

May 6 First cross-country flight by a Bell Boeing V-22 Osprey tilt-rotor transport, flying from Dallas to Wilmington, a distance of 1,393 miles (2,241km). First sea trials by two Ospreys take place on board U.S.S. *Wasp* during December 4–7.

June 10 A British Airways BAC One-Eleven, in the early part of its flight to Malaga, makes an emergency landing at Southampton after a cockpit windscreen blows out at 23,000ft (7,000m), sucking Captain Tim Lancaster half out. Fortunately, having been grabbed by the co-pilot and steward, he was then held by his legs for the 18 minutes it took to land the aircraft.

July 3 The longest straight-line distance flown to date in a hang-glider is set at 303.36 miles (488.2km), between New Mexico and Kansas by American Larry Tudor in a Wills Wing.

August 2 Iraqi forces advance into Kuwait, so beginning the Gulf War.

August 7 2,300 paratroops of the U.S. Army's 82nd Airborne Division are airlifted to Saudi Arabia at the start of Operation *Desert Shield*, the largest-ever military airlift. To protect Saudi Arabia, coalition forces are massed over the coming 22 days, with a C-141B StarLifter, C-5 Galaxy or other aircraft landing at Dhahran every seven minutes (average) in the early days of the operation.

The longest operational deployment of fighters to date is recorded during Operation *Desert Shield*, when 48 U.S.A.F. McDonnell Douglas F-15C/D Eagles of the 27th and 71st TFSs, 1st Tactical Fighter Wing, are flown non-stop from Langley AFB, Virginia to Dhahran, Saudi Arabia, each fighter carrying air-to-air armament and requiring several aerial refuellings.

August 8 The U.S. Navy aircraft carrier U.S.S. *Dwight D. Eisenhower* and battle group station in the Red Sea, while U.S.A.F. Boeing B-52s begin deployment to Diego Garcia in the Indian Ocean. The carrier U.S.S. *John F. Kennedy* sets out for the Gulf on the 15th.

August 9 The United Nations' Security Council pass Resolution 662, requiring Iraqi forces to withdraw from Kuwait.

August 10 The first squadron of R.A.F. aircraft, Panavia Tornado F.Mk 3 interceptors, arrive in Dhahran. R.A.F. SEPECAT Jaguar GR.Mk 1A attack aircraft arrive in Thumrait, Oman, the following day.

August 13 The French Navy aircraft carrier *Clemenceau* sets sail for Djibouti, carrying 42 anti-armour helicopters for the French rapid action force in the Gulf.

August 19 Twenty-one U.S.A.F. F-117A stealth fighters of the 37th TFW leave their base at Tonopah to take part in Operation *Desert Shield* during the Gulf War. After touch-down at Langley, they fly non-stop to the King Khalid Air Base in Saudi Arabia (arriving on the 21st), having been refuelled in mid-air by KC-10A tankers. Others from the 417th TFW arrive between December 4 (1990) and January 26 (1991). (q.v. 1991)

August 25 United Nations' Security Council Resolution 665 is granted, authorizing the use of some force if needed to ensure that the blockade on trade from Iraq and Kuwait is not broken. U.S.S. *Saratoga* takes over from U.S.S. *Dwight D. Eisenhower* in the Gulf. Other aircraft carrier movements followed during the conflict.

August 29 A U.S.A.F. Lockheed C-5A Galaxy heavy transport crashes on take-off in Germany, with the loss of the crew and cargo bound for Saudi Arabia. This is the first non-combat air loss of the Gulf conflict.

September A Ukrainian-built Antonov An-124 is used to emergency airlift 451 refugees from Amman to Dacca.

September 27 On a flight from San Francisco to Hong Kong, United Airlines becomes the first to use satellite data communications on a commercial service.

September 29 First flight of the first of two prototype Lockheed F-22 Advanced Tactical Fighters for the U.S.A.F., from Palmdale to Edwards Air Force Base. The first supersonic flight by an F-22 followed on October 25.

1990 Osprey sea trials on U.S.S. Wasp

October The Cameron combination helium gas and hot-air balloon *Roziere* R-60 makes the first balloon flight from Great Britain to the U.S.S.R.

October 7 As Coalition forces gather under Operation *Desert Shield*, 12 Canadian CF-18 Hornets of No. 419 Squadron arrive in Qatar.

October 18 An R.A.F. Tornado GR.Mk 1 of No. 16 Squadron becomes the first (non-U.S.) Coalition air loss of Operation *Desert Shield* when an arrester barrier catches the landing gear and causes the aircraft to strike the runway. The two crew safely eject and the aircraft is returned to the U.K. for repair.

November 29 United Nations' Security Council Resolution 678 is granted, authorizing the use of force against Iraq unless it withdraws from Kuwait by January 15, 1991.

December 2 U.S. Astronaut Vance DeVoe Brand lifts-off on board Space Shuttle *Columbia*, mission STS 35. At 59, he is the oldest astronaut/cosmonaut to date (still the oldest in 1996).

December 17 U.S. Army General H. Norman Schwarzkopf orders deployment of the two Northrop Grumman E-8A Joint STARS development aircraft to the Gulf for surveillance during the conflict with Iraq. They return to the U.S.A. in March 1991 after flying 535 operational hours in 49 missions with 4411 Squadron.

December 31 The 6,000th life is saved by Martin-Baker ejection seats, when the four crew of a U.S. Navy Grumman EA-6B Prowler of VAQ-141 Squadron from U.S.S. *Theodore Roosevelt* eject safely.

1991

January 13 The first Boeing 727-100 (N7001U, *Spirit of Seattle*) is withdrawn from service, after 64,492 flight hours with United Air Lines.

January 15–17 The fastest speed recorded to date for a manned hot-air balloon is 239mph (385km/h), set by the *Virgin Otsuka Pacific Flyer* crewed by Richard Branson and Per Lindstrand during this first-ever transpacific flight by a hot-air balloon, between Miyakonojo (Japan) and the North West Territories, Canada. The distance covered is 6,761 miles (10,878km), a record (then) for balloons (q.v. January 7, 1997)

January 16 Eight U.S. Army McDonnell Douglas AH-64 Apache attack helicopters of the 101st Airborne Division plus a CH-53 pathfinder, head out to attack two Iraqi air defence radar sites west of Baghdad. These are the first aircraft to take off for an actual attack mission during Operation *Desert Storm*. The Apaches begin their attack at 2.38 am on the 17th, firing Hellfire missiles, rockets and guns, destroying their targets.

January 17 The start of Operation *Desert Storm* (Gulf War), the United Nations/Coalition forces' military action to expel Iraqi forces from Kuwait. (q.v. January 16, 1991)

The first fixed-wing aircraft to take off under Operation *Desert Storm* are U.S.A.F. Lockheed F-117A stealth fighters and U.S.A.F., U.S. Navy and R.A.F. tankers in the early minutes of the 17th, the latter to flight refuel attacking tactical aircraft. The F-117As make the first fixed-wing aircraft attack of Operation *Desert Storm*, striking at air defence installations near Baghdad and a communications centre in Baghdad, the latter at about 03.00 am.

Tomahawk missiles, fired from U.S.S. *Missouri*, *Wisconsin* and *San Jacinto* in the Persian Gulf, hit targets in Baghdad in the very early hours of the 17th.

The first Iraqi Air Force loss of the Gulf War was a Dassault Mirage F1 interceptor that hit the ground during a low-level manoeuvre while attacking a U.S.A.F. Grumman EF-111A Raven electronic warfare aircraft.

The first Coalition victory in air-to-air combat of Operation *Desert Storm* was at about 03.20 am, when Captain Steve Tate flying a McDonnell Douglas F-15C Eagle with the 71st Tactical Fighter Squadron fired a Sparrow missile at an Iraqi Dassault Mirage F1, which was hit.

The U.S. Navy records its first air victories of Operation *Desert Storm* when two bomb-carrying McDonnell Douglas F/A-18C Hornets of VFA-81 claim two Iraqi Mikoyan MiG-21s in air-to-air combat.

Lt. Cmdr. Michael Scott Speicher, flying a McDonnell Douglas F/A-18C Hornet from U.S.S. *Saratoga*, is killed when his aircraft is hit by an SA-6 anti-aircraft missile. This is the first American combat air loss of the Gulf War.

The first (non-U.S.) Coalition air loss of Operation *Desert Storm* was an R.A.F. Panavia Tornado GR.Mk 1 of No. XV Squadron, while mounting an attack on the Shaibah air base. Loss was not caused by combat damage and the crew ejected, to become POWs of Iraq.

January 18 Coalition forces begin the hunt for Iraqi Scud missile launchers, after five (of seven launched) Scuds with conventional warheads hit Israel (other Scud attacks followed). Among many other actions, French Jaguars attack a munitions store at Ras Al Qulayah.

January 19 First operational missions by R.A.F. Tornado GR. Mk 1A reconnaissance aircraft, one of which pinpointed a Scud site for attack.

January 20 Heavy action by Iraqi and Coalition forces includes the launch of two Iraqi Scuds and three Frog surface-to-surface missiles against Saudi Arabia (Scuds intercepted by U.S. Patriot missiles).

January 22 Three Iraqi transport aircraft fly to Iran and out of the conflict. Others follow from the 23rd, with combat types also

leaving from the 26th to avoid destruction in the air or on the ground in their (still vulnerable) hardened shelters.

January 24 Capt. Ayehid Salah al-Shamrani of No. 13 Squadron, Royal Saudi Air Force, records the first non-U.S. victory in air-to-air combat, claiming two Iraqi Mirage F1s, his F-15C Eagle having been guided to the targets by E-3 AWACS.

January 27 Actions include three U.S.A.F. General Dynamics F-111Fs of the 48th TFW attacking two oil pumping stations in Kuwait (in Iraqi hands) with GBU-15 precision bombs that had been releasing a giant oil slick into the Persian Gulf to hinder Coalition naval activities.

January 30 Iraqi ground forces with armoured support launch five separate incursions into Saudi Arabia. After one is detected by an unmanned aerial vehicle, four are stopped by AV-8B, HueyCobra and other counter attacks. One incursion reaches Khafji, where it is attacked by HueyCobras and A-10As.

Naval air actions include Royal Navy Lynx helicopters and U.S. Navy Hornets and Intruders attacking many Iraqi fast patrol boats (a number armed with Exocet anti-ship missiles), causing several to be sunk.

The Coalition claims air supremacy over Iraq.

February 6 Captain Robert Swain of the U.S.A.F.'s 706th Tactical Fighter Squadron, shoots down an Iraqi BO 105 helicopter while flying a Fairchild A-10A Thunderbolt II attack aircraft. On February 15, Captain Todd Sheehy of the 511th TFS shoots down an Iraqi Mil Mi-8 helicopter. Thus, to these A-10As go the unusual distinction of gaining the only gun air-to-air 'victories' of the Gulf War.

February 13 Among other actions, 46 U.S.A.F. General Dynamics F-111Fs of the 48th TFW, each carrying four laser-guided bombs, strike 132 Iraqi armoured vehicles.

February 19 U.S. Navy squadron VS-32, operating Lockheed S-3B Vikings, sinks a patrol boat during Operation *Desert Storm*.

February 23 Reconnaissance shows that Iraqi forces have set alight more than 300 oil wells in Kuwait. Many more will be fired in the coming days.

February 24 Massive Coalition ground forces begin the ground war offensive against Iraqi forces in Kuwait and southern Iraq, supported by heavy air activity.

The largest-ever helicopter-borne attack takes place when more than 2,000 troops of the U.S. Army's 101st Airborne Division are air-lifted by Chinook and Black Hawk helicopters to strategic points during Gulf War, supported by AH-1 HueyCobra, AH-64 Apache and AH-58 Warrior escort gunship helicopters. The total force comprises about 550 helicopters.

February 26 Iraq orders its forces out of Kuwait.

February 28 The end of the Gulf War, with the Coalition air forces having flown over 110,000 sorties, recording the first occasion air power alone had rendered one of the world's largest land armies ineffective, though ground and naval forces had played important roles in the final victory. Since January 17, Iraq has lost 40 aircraft in air combat, with a huge number of others having been either destroyed on the ground or flown to Iran. Coalition combat losses are 35 U.S. aircraft, six R.A.F. Tornados, a Kuwaiti Skyhawk (January 17th) and an Italian Tornado (January 17th), though none were lost in air-to-air combat (many brought down or very badly damaged by ground fire/missiles). Thousands of Iraqi tanks have been destroyed, along with thousands of personnel carriers, artillery pieces and other equipment, radar sites, communications centres and much more.

March 1 Major Marie T. Rossi dies when the Chinook helicopter she is piloting strikes a microwave tower while flying a low-level mission. Having flown troops into action during Operation *Desert Storm*, she is reportedly the highest-ranking American to be killed during the Gulf War and its aftermath.

April 27 First flight of the Eurocopter Tiger (Tigre) anti-armour and combat support helicopter.

May 24 An El Al Boeing 747 airliner with its galleys and all except four toilets removed, carries the largest number of passengers ever recorded on a flight by a commercial airliner, at 1,087. This occurs during Operation *Solomon*, when Falasha people are evacuated to Israel from Ethiopia. The airliner has a staggering 760 seats installed, with six persons occupying every four seats by folding away the armrests. During the flight, three babies are born.

June 1 A Python is found in a baggage locker on board a Delta airliner en route from Orlando.

July 17 A Lockheed S-3B Viking records the longest flight ever made after taking off from an aircraft carrier, at 5,873 miles (9,445km), lasting 15.5 hours.

July 22 American Kari Castle establishes the current world hang gliding distance record for women at 208.66 miles (335.8km), at Owens Valley, California.

September 15 First flight of the McDonnell Douglas C-17A Globemaster III heavy-lift transport for the U.S.A.F. First delivery to an operational unit, the 437th Air Wing, takes place on June 14, 1993, having earlier gone to the 6517th Test Squadron (September 15, 1991).

October 21 Chris Dewhirst and Leo Dickinson in *Star Flyer 1*, together with Andy Elson and Eric Jones in *Star Flyer 2*, make the first balloon flights over the summit of Mount Everest.

1991 Globemaster III dispensing flares

October 25 First flight of the Airbus A340 long-range airliner.

December 4 Following financial difficulties, the original Pan Am airline makes its last commercial flight, flown by a Boeing 727 between Bridgetown, Barbados and Miami. In charge is Captain Mark Pyle.

1992

February Production of the Russian Tupolev Tu-95 *Bear* bomber finally comes to an end.

April 15 First flight of the prototype McDonnell Douglas AH-64D Longbow Apache attack helicopter for the U.S. Army and export.

April 17 Gérard Herbaud and Jean-Noël Herbaud establish a new world distance record for two-seat gliders, flying over 859 miles (1,383km) from Vinon, France to Fez, Morocco in a Schleicher ASH 25 glider.

May 13 Astronauts Rick Hieb, Pierre Thuot and Tom Akers undertake the longest-ever spacewalk (EVA), at 8 hrs 29 mins, during Space Shuttle Endeavour Mission STS 49. It is the first triple spacewalk and recovers the *Intelsat 6*.

June 1 The U.S.A.F. establishes Air Combat Command from the former Tactical Air Command and Strategic Air Command. Headquartered at Langley AFB, it is expected to provide combat air forces that include fighters, bombers, reconnaissance and related aircraft types as well as providing nuclear-capable forces for U.S. Strategic Command.

The U.S.A.F. establishes Air Mobility Command from the former Military Airlift Command, to operate transport and aerial refuelling aircraft. It is the Air Force arm of the U.S. Transportation Command.

July 1 The U.S.A.F. establishes Air Force Materiel Command.

August 26 Dr. Glenn Singleman and Nicholas Feteris make the highest-ever recorded parachute jump from land, leaping from the Great Trango Tower ledge in the Karakoram mountains, Pakistan.

September 10 The first production JAS 39 Gripen fighter flies.

September 12 15 persons parachute from a hot-air balloon flying over Somerset and Devon, U.K. This is the largest number ever to parachute from a balloon.

September 22 First flight of the all-weather, day-and-night-attack, and air-to-air STOVL-capable McDonnell Douglas/BAe Harrier II Plus, with Hughes APG-65 multi-mode radar.

September 16–22 Americans Richard Abruzzo and Troy Bradley set a new world duration record for balloons, by flying for 144 hrs 16 mins in the Cameron R77 *Team USA*, from Bangor, Maine, U.S.A. to Ben Slimane, Morocco.

October 1–2 American Maynard Hill sets the current world record for the longest endurance flight by a model aircraft, at 33 hrs 39 mins 15 secs.

October 7 Sea deployment starts on board the aircraft carrier U.S.S. *John F. Kennedy* of Northrop Grumman F-14A Tomcats converted for bombing, known unofficially as Bombats. (The last newly built F-14 of any version was delivered to the U.S. Navy on July 20, as a F-14D.)

October 22 Russian Kh-55 *Kent* advanced cruise missiles are launched for the first time from a Tupolev Tu-160.

October 23 The current FAI official world record for the largest-ever free-fall formation is set at 200 persons, at an altitude of 16,500ft (5,000m) over South Carolina, U.S.A. (q.v. August 19, 1994)

November 2 First flight of the Airbus A330 medium-range wide-body airliner.

December 1 Briton Judy Leden establishes the current world height-gain hang gliding record for women at 13,025ft (3,970m), at Kuruman, South Africa.

December 14 61 refugees are killed in a Russian helicopter, shot down over Georgia. This is the world's worst helicopter loss.

December 29 Certification is gained for the Russian Ilyushin Il-96 wide-body airliner, having first flown on September 28, 1988.

1993

January 6 Briton Robby Whittal sets a paragliding height-gain record (after towed launch) at Brandvlei, South Africa, of 14,850ft (4,526m).

January 13 Major Susan Helms, U.S.A.F., is launched on Space Shuttle *Endeavour*. She is the first American military woman to enter space.

January 22 Briton Robby Whittal sets a distance paragliding record from Kuruman, South Africa, of 157 miles (253km). (q.v. December 25, 1995 for towed)

March 11 First flight of the Airbus A321 airliner.

March 19 First known loss of a Sukhoi Su-27 in combat, hit by a surface-to-air missile over Sukhumi.

July 13 The new Russian Beriev Be-12P fire-fighting conversion of the military ASW and SAR amphibian drops 248 tons (252 tonnes) of water in just two runs to tackle a fire at the village of Listvianka.

September An Antonov An-124-100 carries the heaviest single load ever airlifted (to date), comprising a 122-ton (124tonne) power

1992 Airbus A330

1993 An-124-100 with 133-ton payload

plant generator core plus its load-spreading skid, totalling 133 tons (135.2 tonnes), transported from Düsseldorf in Germany to New Delhi in India.

December 2–13 U.S. Space Shuttle *Endeavour* undertakes a successful mission to repair the Hubble Space Telescope.

December 11 The first production Northrop Grumman B-2A Spirit (AV-8 *Missouri*) stealth bomber is delivered to the 509th Bomb Wing at Whiteman Air Force Base.

1994
January 25 The unmanned *Clementine* spacecraft is launched on the first American lunar mission since the Apollo flights.

February 7 The first U.S. *Milstar* satellite is launched into orbit.

March 27 First flight of the first Eurofighter development aircraft (DA1) at Manching, Germany. (q.v. December 23, 1997)

April 10 Under Operation *Blue Sword* NATO air forces, for the first time in the history of the organization, undertake their first air strikes against ground targets when two U.S.A.F. F-16Cs drop bombs on a Bosnian Serb artillery command centre, following the shelling (by a tank) of the Moslem sector of Gorazde.

June 12 First flight of the Boeing 777 long-range wide-body airliner.

June 2–July 22 American Ron Bower sets the current world record for the fastest around-the-world flight by helicopter. Using a Bell

206B-3 JetRanger, he left Fort Worth on the 28th and took 24 days 4 hrs 36 mins 24 secs, flying eastward, with 81 stopovers en route.

June 29 An American Space Shuttle first flies to a Russian *Mir* space station.

August Two U.S.A.F. Boeing B-52 bombers from Barksdale Air Force Base undertake the first around-the-world bombing mission, releasing 27,000lb (12,250kg) of bombs in the Kuwait desert during a 47-hour practice mission.

August 19 216 persons perform the largest-ever free-fall formation (though not officially recognized as a record), at an altitude of 21,000ft (6,400m) over Slovakia. (q.v. October 23, 1992)

September 18 A world altitude record for microlights is set by Frenchman Serge Zin, who reaches 31,890ft (9,720m) over St.-Auban, France.

October 6–11 A Beriev Be-12NKh civil transport conversion of the Be-12 (q.v. July 13, 1993) delivers 29.5 tons (30 tonnes) of supplies to earthquake victims in Yuzhno-Kurilsk.

October 12 At Davis, California, 46 persons perform a parachute canopy stack lasting over 37 seconds, the greatest number so far recorded.

October 19 First flight of a Boeing 767 AWACS aircraft, prior to having its specialized equipment fitted. (It first flies after 'fitting out' on August 9, 1996 and delivery will take place in March 1998.)

November 5 The *Ulysses* spacecraft passes over the Sun's southern pole.

December 16 First flight of the Ukrainian Antonov An-70 medium freighter.

December 28 First flight of the Russian Sukhoi Su-32FN long-range maritime strike aircraft.

1995
Alaska Airlines becomes the first U.S. airline to book travel and sell tickets via the Internet. Previously, in 1989, it had been the first airline in the world to manually land a passenger jet in FAA Category III weather conditions, using a revolutionary 'fog busting' head-up flight guidance system; in 1990 an Alaska Boeing 727 with the guidance system became the first passenger jet to take off in under 600ft (183m) of runway visibility.

February 6 The U.S. Space Shuttle *Discovery*, on Mission STS 63, joins the Russian *Mir* space station in space, the first U.S.-Russian rendezvous for two decades. *Discovery* is piloted by U.S.A.F. Lt. Col. Eileen Collins, the first woman to pilot an American spacecraft. (q.v. June 29, 1995)

February 17–21 Steve Fossett establishes a new world distance record for balloons by flying a Cameron R-150 from Seoul, South Korea to Mendham, Saskatchewan, Canada, a distance of over 5,435 miles (8,748km). This is also the first solo balloon flight across the Pacific. (q.v. 1997)

March 14 Astronaut Norman Thagard is the first American to be launched with Russian cosmonauts on board *Soyuz TM21*. On the

16th he enters the Russian space station *Mir*, the first American to do so. The 14th also marks the occasion when the largest number of astronauts and cosmonauts are in space at the same time, comprising the seven crew of U.S. Space Shuttle *Endeavour* (Mission STS 67), two cosmonauts and an American on board Russian *Soyuz TM21*, and three cosmonauts on the *Mir* space station.

March 22 Russian cosmonaut Dr. Valeriy Poliyakov returns to Earth on board *Soyuz TM20* after the longest-ever spaceflight lasting 437 days 17 hrs 58 mins 16 secs. Launched on *Soyuz TM18* on January 8, 1994, most of the time had been spent on the *Mir* space station.

April 4 The British Government announces that the R.A.F. will end its nuclear capability in 1998 when WE177 free-fall nuclear bombs are finally withdrawn.

June 2 A U.S.A.F. F-16 on patrol in the 'no-fly zone' over Bosnia is brought down by a Bosnian Serb anti-aircraft missile. After six days of avoiding capture, the pilot, Capt. Scott O'Grady of the 555th Fighter Squadron, is rescued by U.S.M.C. CH-53 helicopters from the assault ship U.S.S. *Kearsage*, supported by attack helicopters and warplanes.

June 26 Americans Robert Rosenthal and Maynard Hill establish the current world distance record for model aircraft flying in a closed circuit, at 776 miles (1,250km).

June 29 U.S. Space Shuttle *Atlantis*, on Mission STS 71, docks with the Russian *Mir* space station, the first-ever docking of a U.S. spacecraft with a Russian space station.

July The largest radio-controlled model aircraft in the world flies as a scale-model of the Ukrainian Antonov An-225 Mriya. Constructor is Briton Simon Cocker.

August 4 The Grob G 850 Strato 2C sets a new world altitude record for manned piston-engined aircraft, at 60,867ft (18,552m).

August 5 A Delta II booster launches South Korea's *Koreasat-1* communications satellite into space.

August 10 First flight of the Indonesian IPTN N-250 regional airliner.

August 11 First flight of the Brazilian EMBRAER EMB-145 regional jet airliner.

August 15–16 An Air France Concorde supersonic airliner, flown by Michel Dupont and Claude Hetru and carrying 96 other persons, sets a speed record for flying around the world at over 811mph (1,305km/h). The elapsed time is a record 31 hrs 27 mins 49 secs.

August 16 American Col. Clarence Cornish flies a Cessna 172, making him the world's oldest pilot, at 96. He first flew in 1918.

August 25 First flight of the Airbus A319 short/medium-range airliner.

August 30 Under Operation *Deliberate Force*, NATO aircraft under the sanction of the United Nations begin the first large-scale attacks on Bosnian Serb air defence, radar, communications, ammunition and other targets, following a Serbian mortar attack on Sarajevo on the 28th (37 civilians killed) and some three years of hostilities in the region. (Earlier NATO raids, such as those in November 1994 and May 1995, had been on a much smaller scale.) A French Dassault Mirage 2000N is shot down by an SA-7 ground-launched missile.

September 1 The German Luftwaffe undertakes its first combat mission since the end of the Second World War when a Panavia Tornado ECR reconnaissance aircraft of JBG 32 flies a reconnaissance sortie over former Yugoslavia from a base in Italy, in support of United Nations' Operation *Deliberate Force*.

October 7 First flight of the Japanese Mitsubishi F-2 (then known as FS-X) close support and anti-shipping fighter.

October 20 The astronauts on U.S. Space Shuttle *Columbia*, on Mission STS 73, undertake microgravity experiments, useful for possible future chemical and pharmaceutical manufacturing.

November 8–9 American Cheryl Stearns sets the current world record for the greatest number of parachute jumps in 24 hours, at 352, from Raeford, North Carolina.

November 12–20 U.S. Space Shuttle *Atlantis*, on Mission STS-74,

1996 Boeing Sikorsky RAH-66 Comanche

makes the second Shuttle docking with the Russian *Mir* space station. The Shuttle carries food and water to *Mir*.

November 17 Roll-out of the prototype Indian Light Combat Aircraft at Bangalore.

December In the Russian Navy's first major deployment into the Adriatic and the first operational deployment of its new aircraft carrier, *Admiral Kuznetsov*, it and escorting ships assist in supporting the Bosnia peace agreement.

December 2 A U.S. Atlas IIAS rocket launches the European Space Agency's *Solar and Heliospheric Observatory* into orbit.

December 7 The *Galileo* satellite, launched by U.S. Space Shuttle *Atlantis* in 1989, launches a parachute probe into Jupiter's atmosphere.

December 18 First flight of the NHIndustries NH90 tactical transport helicopter.

December 25 British woman K. Thurston sets a new (and current) paragliding distance record after a towed launch from Kuruman in South Africa, of 177 miles (285km).

December 28 China uses its Long March booster rocket to launch the American *EchoStar-1* direct-broadcast satellite.

1996

January 4 First flight of the Boeing Sikorsky RAH-66 Comanche battlefield helicopter, intended for U.S. Army service from 2006.

January 11–20 U.S. Space Shuttle Mission STS 72, using *Endeavour*, retrieves the Japanese Space Flyer Unit satellite among other objectives.

February American Nicholas Piantanida sets an unofficial world altitude record at 123,800ft (37,735m) for piloted balloons. Having taken off from Sioux Falls, South Dakota, he was killed during the landing in Iowa.

February 17 American Hildegarde Ferrera becomes the oldest person ever to make a tandem parachute jump, at the age of 99 (over Mokuleia, Hawaii).

February 26 U.S. Space Shuttle *Columbia* fully deploys the Italian Tethered Satellite during Mission STS 75. With the tether extending more than 12 miles (19km) from the Shuttle, the combined shuttle/satellite becomes the largest-ever object in space.

March 15 Fokker of the Netherlands is declared bankrupt, having been an aircraft manufacturer since 1919. Various revival attempts follow.

March 21 First flight of the Russian Tupolev Tu-214 airliner.

March 22 U.S. Space Shuttle *Atlantis* lifts off on Mission STS 76 carrying American Shannon Lucid, at 53 the oldest woman astronaut to date. Spending 181 days on board the Russian *Mir* space station before returning to Earth on Shuttle Mission STS-79 in November 1996, she establishes a new endurance record for an American living in space and broke the world's record for a woman

in space. She received the U.S. Congressional Space Medal of Honor in December. Mission STS-76 itself lasts until March 30, and includes the first Shuttle-*Mir* EVA.

March 31 Delta Air Lines establishes a world record when the 2-millionth passenger boarded a Delta flight at Hartsfield Atlanta International Airport, the first occasion this number of passengers had ever been recorded at a single airport during one month.

April 5 First flight of the C-130J Hercules, the latest version of this long-serving transport. (q.v. August 26,1998)

May The first edition of *Brassey's World Aircraft & Systems Directory* is published, conceived and edited by Michael J. H. Taylor. Formerly the Assistant Editor on *Jane's All the World's Aircraft*, Michael Taylor conceived *Brassey's WA&SD* to be the world's most comprehensive aviation work.

American Don Kellner records his 22,000th parachute jump, the greatest-ever number for one person.

May 30 French Armée de l'Air Dassault Mirage IV-P nuclear-armed strategic bombers fly their last mission, so ending 33 years of service (originally as IV-As). The Bretagne operating unit is disbanded at Cazaux on July 4. The five strategic reconnaissance conversions will continue operations until 2005.

June The Saab JAS 39A Gripen combat aircraft is officially accepted into the Swedish Air Force with a ceremony at F7 Wing.

June 24 The 5,000th aircraft of the Beech King Air range is delivered to a customer.

July 27 After a long and distinguished career, General Dynamics F-111 fighter-bombers are finally retired from the U.S.A.F. (with the exception of Grumman EF-111A Raven electronic warfare conversions).

August 6 First flight of the Japanese Kawasaki OH-X armed scout and observation helicopter, also capable of attack. Production began in mid-1998 as the OH-1 Kogata Kansoku.

September 3 In Operation *Desert Strike*, the U.S. Navy launches 14 Tomahawk cruise missiles from two ships and the U.S.A.F. launches 13 AGM-86C cruise missiles from two Boeing B-52Hs against air defence and command/control centre targets in southern Iraq following Iraq's assault on the town of Arbil in northern Iraq on August 30. The B-52s had flown from Guam, making a 34-hour and 27,000-mile (43,450km) round flight. A further 17 Tomahawks are launched from three destroyers and a submarine on the 4th.

October 17 The last airworthy Vickers Vanguard makes its final flight, landing at the Brooklands Museum.

1996 First C-130J Hercules

1996 118C. JAS 39A Gripen of F7 Wing

November 12 A Saudia Boeing 747 and a Kazakhstan Airlines Ilyushin Il-76TD collide near New Delhi, India. The 312 crew and passengers of the 747 and 39 of the Il-76TD are killed or die from their injuries.

November 29 First flight of the upgraded Russian Tupolev Tu-144LL supersonic airliner at Zhukovsky. With new engines, it will be used for research into the next generation of supersonic airliners on behalf of NASA and various U.S. and U.K. companies.

December 15 It is announced that Boeing is to take over McDonnell Douglas in a $13.3 billion agreement, creating the world's largest aerospace company.

December 19 U.S. Navy Grumman A-6E Intruders complete their last-ever operational deployment, so ending the 34-year career of this strike bomber. The final 14 A-6Es of VA-75 had been on board U.S.S. *Enterprise* and are being replaced by Hornets.

1997

January Boeing, the world's largest producer of commercial aircraft, announces that orders for the 737, the world's best-selling airliner in history, have exceeded 3,600.

January 4 A Hong Kong newspaper reports that China is likely to have its first aircraft carrier completed by the year 2000, a full five years earlier than expected.

January 6 Airbus Industrie announces plans to virtually double production of its airliners over the coming two years.

January 7 The 194.88ft (59.4m) total height, 1.1 million cu ft (31,148m³) combined helium gas and hot air balloon *Virgin Global Challenger* lifts off from Marrakech in Morocco at 11.19 am to attempt the first non-stop circumnavigation of the world by balloon. On board are Richard Branson, Per Lindstrand and Alex Ritchie. The balloon rises far more quickly than anticipated, reaching its 30,000-ft (9,150m) maximum altitude in just an hour, thereafter making a series of very rapid descents, causing near disaster. The attempt ends at 07.20 am on January 8 at Bechar in Algeria.

January 12 *Breitling Orbiter* lifts off from Chateau O'Oex in Switzerland in an attempt to make the first non-stop circumnavigation of the world by balloon. Crewed by Swiss Bertrand Piccard and Belgian Wim Verstraeten, the flight finishes in a controlled landing in the Mediterranean just six hours later, after kerosene fumes had leaked into the crew capsule.

January 14–20 American J. Stephen Fossett (aged 52) takes off from St. Louis, Missouri, U.S.A., in his 170-ft (52m) high helium gas/hot-air balloon Cameron R-210 *Solar Spirit*, in an attempt to make the first non-stop circumnavigation of the world by balloon. Flying alone, he is forced to use more fuel than anticipated and

lands 6 days 2 hrs and 54 mins later at Nonkhar, Sultan Par, India, having failed to fly around the world but having broken his own world endurance record for ballooning by 1 hr 38 mins. The distance flown of 10,360 miles (16,673km) is also a record.

January 31 This date sees the decommissioning of Indian Navy aircraft carrier I.N.S. *Vikrant*.

February 1 The new aircraft carrier *Charles de Gaulle* is handed over to the French Navy. Still undergoing fitting out, it will enter operational service in 1999.

March 14 Last official flight of the final airworthy de Havilland Comet (XS235 *Canopus*) takes place at Boscombe Down. This Comet 4C was first flown in 1963 and has been used for research duties.

April 1 Initial operational capability is achieved by the Northrop Grumman B-2A Spirit bomber, with 393rd Bomb Squadron of the 509th Bomb Wing.

May 17 An ex-Air France Boeing 747-128 dating from 1971 is deliberately destroyed by four remotely detonated explosions at Bruntingthorpe Airfield in Leicestershire as part of the Civil Aircraft Explosion Hardening Project to improve airliner safety against terrorist threats.

June 25 First flight of the Russian Kamov Ka-52 Alligator *Hokum-B* two-seat combat helicopter, flown by Alexander Smirnov and Dmitri Titov.

July 8–9 AV-15 *Alaska* makes the longest Northrop Grumman B-2A stealth bomber flight to date, of 25 hrs 30 mins.

August 4 Boeing and McDonnell Douglas begin operating as a merged company, under the Boeing name.

August 8 First flight of the Zeppelin NT series LZ N 07 rigid helium airship demonstrator.

August 14 The U.S.A.F. retires its last Lockheed T-33, an NT-33A in-flight simulator aircraft. It had undertaken its final mission on April 22.

September 7 First flight of a Lockheed Martin F-22 Raptor EMD prototype, piloted by Paul Metz.

September 25 First flight of the Russian Sukhoi S-37 fifth-generation tactical fighter, piloted by Igor Votintsev. S-37 features forward-swept wings.

December 23 Eurofighter DA2 makes the first Mach 2 flight of the Eurofighter test programme. The first in-flight refuelling is demonstrated in January 1998.

1997 Virgin Global Challenger *(courtesy Virgin)*

1997 F-22 Raptor EMD prototype

1998

January 28–February 7 A new world duration record for free-flying balloons is established by Bertrand Piccard of Switzerland and Andy Elson of the U.K. in the Cameron gas/hot-air balloon *Breitling Orbiter 2*, flying from Château d'Oex, Switzerland to Sitkwin Minhla, Myanmar. The record set is 233 hrs 55 mins.

February 28 First flight of the Teledyne Ryan RQ-4A Global Hawk unmanned air vehicle reconnaissance aircraft.

March 28 The Chinese Nanchang Aircraft Manufacturing Company changes its name to Hongdu Aviation Industry Group.

April 1 The Royal Air Force becomes a fully non-nuclear force as the WE177 tactical nuclear weapon is withdrawn earlier than expected from first-line service by the Labour Government's Defence Secretary.

April 27 The U.S.A.F. announces that the Lockheed SR-71 Blackbird supersonic strategic reconnaissance aircraft is to remain retired from operational use.

May 19 Dassault Aviation of France presents the design concept for a 2-crew and 8-passenger supersonic Falcon business jet, to be capable of cruising at Mach 1.8 and have a range of 4,000 nautical miles.

May 31 Boeing announces that since the beginning of the year it has received orders worth US$15.459 billion, having a backlog of 1,793 aircraft to deliver.

June 24 The U.S.S. *Harry S. Truman* (CVN-75) nuclear-powered aircraft carrier completes its acceptance sea trials. It is to be commissioned by the U.S. Navy the following month.

July 4 The prototype EMBRAER RJ135 (ERJ135) 37-passenger regional jet flies. Production deliveries are then expected to begin in October 1999.

July 15 First flight of the initial production Beech T-6A Texan II trainer, 711 having been ordered for the U.S.A.F. and U.S. Navy under the JPATS programme.

July 26 First flight of the uniquely configured tandem-wing Scaled Composites Proteus proof-of-concept sensor platform aircraft, with future roles to include communications relay, remote sensing and monitoring.

July 30 The 98,000lb (435.93kN) thrust Pratt & Whitney PW4098 turbofan, the world's most powerful commercial aircraft engine intended for the Boeing 777, receives its Type and Production certificates from the FAA.

August 26 First delivery of a Lockheed Martin C-130J Hercules takes place to the R.A.F. as a C-130J-30.

1997 Eurofighter DA2

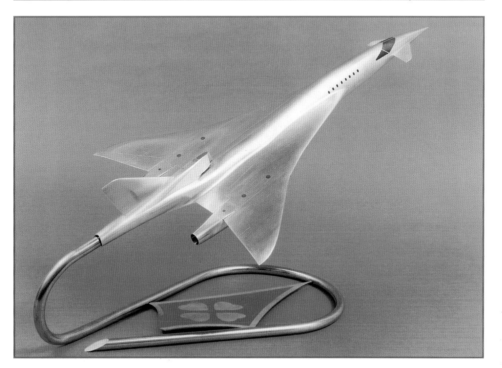
1998 Dassault supersonic Falcon (courtesy Dassault/Aviaplans J.P. Soton)

September 2 Boeing first flies its new Model 717 at Long Beach Airport, having been designed as the McDonnell Douglas MD-95.

September 14 Israel records the first successful launch of its Arrow 2 anti-ballistic missile missile.

September 18 Contracts are signed by Eurofighter GmbH, Eurojet GmbH and NETMA for production of the first 148 Eurofighters.

September 24 First flight of the Russian Beriev Be-200 twin-turbofan amphibian from Irkutsk.

September 25 The first production WAH-64 Apache helicopter for the British Army flies. It is one of eight being built by Boeing prior to British assembly.

September 25 The U.S. Navy assumes responsibility for the command, control and communications of U.S. strategic nuclear forces under the *Looking Glass* role, using E-6B Tacamo aircraft. This role had, up to today, been the responsibility of the U.S.A.F. using now retired C3 variants of the EC-135s.

September 28 The last newly-built Panavia Tornado is delivered. Going to the Royal Saudi Air Force, it marks the end of production after 974 aircraft.

September 30 H.M.S. *Ocean*, the British Royal Navy's new helicopter carrier, is commissioned. It will carry 12 EH 101s and six Lynx, or can instead deploy (but not operationally support) up to 20 Sea Harriers.

October 7 King Harald of Norway opens a new airport at Gardermoen, Oslo. The same day the final flight from the old Fornebu airport is recorded.

October 24 NASA's Deep Space 1 (DS1) technology demonstrator spacecraft is launched from Cape Kennedy in Florida, U.S.A., by a Delta II booster. DS1 has a xenon ion propulsion system.

October 29 Launch of U.S. Space Shuttle mission STS 95 using *Discovery*, the crew including 77-year-old John Glenn. (q.v .February 20, 1962)

November Airbus Industrie announces that it has delivered 1,840 airliners of 3,142 ordered, leaving a backlog of 1,302 to deliver.

November 15 Air attacks on Iraq by U.S. and U.K. aircraft are aborted just 14 minutes before the first attacking aircraft, six U.S.A.F. Boeing B-52H Stratofortresses, were to launch cruise missiles. Other airborne aircraft, including U.S. Navy F-14 Tomcats and F/A-18 Hornets and U.S.A.F. A-10 Thunderbolts and F-16s, are also airborne at the time. Recall is due to a diplomatic solution found at the last possible moment, when Iraq agrees to fully co-operate with United Nations weapon inspectors following diplomatic efforts by Kofi Annan, U.N. Secretary-General. However, in December, further difficulties lead to scaled-down air attacks by U.S. and U.K. forces.

November 20 Assembly of the International Space Station begins, with the launch of Russia's *Zarya* control module from Baikonur. The first module to be attached to *Zarya* is the U.S. Node 1/Unity, carried into space in December on board U.S. space shuttle *Endeavour* on mission STS 88. (q.v. December 10, 1998)

December 10 Astronauts from *Endeavour* connect the first two modules of the International Space Station. (q.v. November 20, 1998), allowing the doors to be opened for the first time and preparing the way for the first occupants in 1999.

December 18 Richard Branson, Steve Fossett and Per Lindstrand lift off from Marrakech at the start of Branson's fourth attempt to circumnavigate the world in a balloon, the *ICO Global Challenger*. The attempt ends short of its goal on the 25th.

December 22 First flight of the Raytheon Premier I business aircraft from Beech Field which lasted 62 minutes.

December 23 First flight of the Sikorsky S-92A Helibus civil and military medium helicopter.

1999

March Publication of the 1999/2000 edition of *Brassey's World Aircraft & Systems Directory*, considered by many to be the world's most comprehensive aviation reference book.

May Anticipated U.S. space shuttle mission STS 96 using *Discovery*, intended for logistics supply to the International Space Station.

July Anticipated launch by Russia of the International Space Station's service module.

March 1–21 *Breitling Orbiter 3*, crewed by Bertrand Piccard of Switzerland and Brian Jones of Great Britain, becomes the first balloon to complete a round-the-world flight. Take-off was from Château d'Oex in Switzerland on March 1, and the balloon finally landed on March 21 in Egypt, at a point some 45 miles (70km) from Mut.

March 25 NATO forces and ship-launched cruise missiles strike at military targets in Serbia, in an attempt to halt the conflict in Kosovo and force a political solution to a long-standing crisis.

1998 EMBRAER RJ135

1998 Raytheon Premier I